D1475310

# UCLA

Los Angeles, CA

*Written by Suzy Strutner, Erik Robert Flegal*

*Edited by the College Prowler Team*

ISBN # 978-1-4274-0612-5

©Copyright 2011 College Prowler

Last updated: 3/24/2011

College Prowler®
5001 Baum Blvd.
Suite 750
Pittsburgh, PA 15213

Phone: (800) 290-2682
Fax: (800) 772-4972
E-Mail: info@collegeprowler.com
Web: www.collegeprowler.com

# How this all started...

When I was trying to find the perfect college, I used every resource that was available to me. I went online to visit school Web sites; I talked with my high school guidance counselor; I read book after book; I hired a private counselor. Sure, this was all very helpful, but nothing really told me what life was like at the schools I cared about. These sources weren't giving me enough information to be totally confident in my decision.

In all my research, there were only two ways to get the information I wanted.

The first was to physically visit the campuses and see if things were really how the brochures described them, but this was quite expensive and not always feasible. The second involved a missing ingredient: the students. Actually talking to a few students at those schools gave me a taste of the information that I needed so badly. The problem was that I wanted more but  didn't have access to enough people.

In the end, I weighed my options and decided on a school that felt right and had a great academic reputation, but truth be told, the choice was still very much a crapshoot. I had done as much research as any other student, but was I 100 percent positive that I had picked the school of my dreams?

Absolutely not.

My dream in creating College Prowler was to build a resource that people can use with confidence. My own college search experience taught me the importance of gaining true insider insight; that's why the majority of this guide is composed of quotes from actual students. After all, shouldn't you hear about a school from the people who know it best?

I hope you enjoy reading this book as much as we've enjoyed putting it together. Tell me what you think when you get a chance. I'd love to hear your college selection stories.

**Luke Skurman**
CEO and Co-Founder
luke@collegeprowler.com

# Welcome to College Prowler®

When we created College Prowler, we felt it was critical that our content was unbiased and unaffiliated with any college or university. We think it's important that our readers get honest information and a realistic impression of the student opinions on any campus—that's why if any aspect of a particular school is terrible, we (unlike a campus brochure) intend to publish it. While we do keep an eye out for the occasional extremist—the cheerleader or the cynic—we take pride in letting the students tell it like it is. We strive to create a book that's as representative as possible of each particular campus. Our books cover both the good and the bad, and whether the survey responses point to recurring trends or a variation in opinion, these sentiments are directly and proportionally expressed through our guides.

College Prowler guidebooks are in the hands of students throughout the entire process of their creation. Because you can't make student-written guides without the students, we have students at each campus who help write, randomly survey their peers, edit, layout, and perform accuracy checks on every book that we publish. From the very beginning, student writers gather the most up-to-date stats, facts, and inside information on their colleges. They fill each section with student quotes and summarize the findings in editorial reviews. In addition, each school receives a collection of letter grades (A through F) that reflect student opinion and help to represent contentment or satisfaction for each of our 20 specific categories. Just as in grade school, the higher the mark the more content or more satisfied the students are with the particular category.

Each book is the result of endless student contributions, hundreds of pages of research and writing, and countless hours of hard work. All of this has led to the creation of a student information network that stretches across the nation to every school that we cover. It's no easy accomplishment, but it's the reason that our guides are such a great resource.

When reading our books and looking at our grades, keep in mind that every college is different and that the students who make up each school are not uniform—as a result, it is important to assess schools on a case-by-case basis. Because it's impossible to summarize an entire school with a single number or description, each book provides a dialogue, not a decision, that's made up of 20 different topics and hundreds of student quotes. In the end, we hope that this guide will serve as a valuable tool in your college selection process. Enjoy!

*The College Prowler Team*

# Table of Contents

# By the Numbers

## School Contact

University of California - Los Angeles
405 Hilgard Ave
Los Angeles, CA 90095

**Control:**
Public

**Academic Calendar:**
Quarter

**Religious Affiliation:**
None

**Founded:**
1919

**Web Site:**
*www.ucla.edu*

**Main Phone:**
(310) 825-4321

## Student Body

**Full-Time Undergraduates:**
25,634

**Part-Time Undergraduates:**
922

**Total Male Undergraduates:**
12,885

**Total Female Undergraduates:**
16,020

## Admissions

**Acceptance Rate:**
23%

**Total Applicants:**
55,423

**Total Acceptances:**
12,659

**Freshman Enrollment:**
4,735

**Yield (% of admitted students who enroll):**
37%

**Transfer Applications Received:**
16,587

**Transfer Applications Accepted:**
5,261

**Transfer Students Enrolled:**
3,235

**Transfer Application Acceptance Rate:**
32%

**SAT I or ACT Required?**
Either

**SAT I Range (25th–75th Percentile):**
1730–2100

**SAT I Verbal Range (25th–75th Percentile):**
560–680

**SAT I Math Range (25th–75th Percentile):**
590–720

**SAT I Writing Range (25th–75th Percentile):**
580–700

**ACT Composite Range (25th–75th Percentile):**
24–31

**ACT English Range (25th–75th Percentile):**
24–32

**ACT Math Range (25th–75th Percentile):**
25–33

**Top 10% of High School Class:**
97%

**Application Fee:**
$60

**Common Application Accepted?**
No

**Admissions Phone:**
(310) 825-3101

**Admissions E-Mail:**
*ugadm@saonet.ucla.edu*

**Admissions Web Site:**
*www.admissions.ucla.edu*

**Regular Decision Deadline:**
November 30

**Regular Decision Notification:**
March 31

**Must-Reply-By Date:**
May 1

# Financial Information

**In-State Tuition:**
$8,266

**Out-of-State Tuition:**
$30,935

**Room and Board:**
$13,310

**Books and Supplies:**
$1,598

**Average Amount of Federal Grant Aid:**
$3,790

**Percentage of Students Who Received Federal Grant Aid:**
31%

**Average Amount of Institution Grant Aid:**
$7,433

**Percentage of Students Who Received Institution Grant Aid:**
51%

**Average Amount of State Grant Aid:**
$3,215

**Percentage of Students Who Received State Grant Aid:**
31%

**Average Amount of Student Loans:**
$4,626

**Percentage of Students Who Received Student Loans:**
33%

**Total Need-Based Package:**
$15,646

**Percentage of Students Who Received Any Aid:**
59%

**Financial Aid Forms Deadline:**
March 2

**Financial Aid Phone:**
(310) 206-0400

**Financial Aid E-Mail:**
*finaid@saonet.ucla.edu*

**Financial Aid Web Site:**
*www.fao.ucla.edu*

# Academics

**The Lowdown On...**
## Academics

### Degrees Awarded
Bachelor's degree
Master's degree

### Most Popular Majors
Business Administration and Management
History, General
Political Science and Government, General
Psychology

### Majors Offered
Architecture and Planning
Arts
Biological Sciences
Business
Computer and Sciences
Education
Engineering
Environmental Sciences
Health Care
Languages and Literature
Law
Mathematics & Statistics
Philosophy and Religion
Physical Sciences

Psychology & Counseling
Social Sciences & Liberal Arts
Social Services

## Undergraduate Schools/Divisions

College of Letters and
Science
Henry Samueli School of
Engineering and Applied
Science
Herb Alpert School of Music
School of Nursing
School of the Arts and
Architecture
School of Theater, Film, and
Television

## Full-Time Instructional Faculty

1,774

## Part-Time Instructional Faculty

508

## Faculty with Terminal Degree

98%

## Average Faculty Salary

$121,306

## Student-Faculty Ratio

17:1

## Class Sizes

Fewer than 20 students: 54%
20 to 49 students: 26%
50 or more students: 20%

## Full-Time Retention Rate

97%

## Part-Time Retention Rate

83%

## Graduation Rate

89%

## Remedial Services?

No

## Academic/Career Counseling?

Yes

## Instructional Programs

Occupational: Yes
Academic: Yes
Continuing Professional: Yes
Recreational/Avocational: No
Adult Basic Remedial: No
Secondary (High School): No

## Special Credit Opportunities

Advanced Placement (AP)

Credits: Yes
Dual Credit: Yes
Life Experience Credits: Yes

## Special Study Options
Distance learning
opportunities
Study abroad

## Other Academic Offerings
Accelerated program
Double major
Honors program
Independent study
Internships
Student-designed major

## Graduation Requirements
English (including
composition)

## Best Places to Study

On the hill next to the Janss Steps
The Powell Library Reading Room
Young Research Library, fourth and fifth floors

## Online Courses

It's rare that students take online courses, but if they want to, they'll encounter a plethora of online options. The UCLA Extension program is reasonably priced and offers a range of classes that bolster most majors; however, those studying more offbeat topics should register for old-fashioned lectures. Classes are taught by "instructors," some of whom are UCLA faculty, and most involve reading online lectures and completing one assignment per week.

## Did You Know?

Bruins can choose from 127 majors, including the newly introduced ethnomusicology major, the only one of its kind in the United States.

You can create your own major by running it over with your counselor and pushing through a lot of red tape. Some of these majors catch on and become entrenched in the curriculum, like the international development major.

Unique general education "clusters" are year-long courses that allow students to knock out a substantial hunk of general ed requirements while bonding with classmates and attending an array of hilarious-sounding field trips, such as fossil hunting in Nevada.

### Students Speak Out On...
# Academics

### Q Psychology Is the Biggest Department on Campus, and for Good Reason

Though many students are put off by the application process for psychology, this department has some of the most interesting classes and professors at UCLA. There are also plenty of research opportunities for undergrads, and professors are usually more than happy to interact with students on a personal level.

### Q Small in Such a Big Campus

Being a French major at UCLA is very unique due to the fact that most people here are majoring in psychology or sociology. The French classes are very small, as is the French department. I love French so I do not really mind how big the program is. I feel very special when I tell everyone that I am a French major because I love it.

### Q Great School

UCLA offers an amazing array of knowledgeable professors that catered to their student's needs.

### Q Big Campus, Yet Never Felt Lost

Academics within UCLA are amazing, I haven't had a professor yet that isn't passionate about the subjects and the students. Most classes are divided into lecture and discussion, which really helps big lectures. Powel Library is just beautiful!

### Q North vs. South

Despite the raging jokes, UCLA truly is divided between North and South campus majors. North campus (liberal arts) majors work hard, but if they manage their time well, they have plenty of opportunities for a social life. South campus majors (science, math, engineering, and pre-med) have a more rigorous course load that is also more structured in terms of what classes they're required to take.

## Q Hard Classes Mean Good Degrees

As a science major, I feel like I go to a different school than the Humanities kids. We do a lot more work, but everyone bonds because of it. No matter your major, the quarter system flies by, so it's very important to go to class.

## Q Pretty Nice

Especially as a freshman, you're amazed at everything amazing the UCLA professors are doing. However, it seems like all the classes are HUGE and the professor only has 1-3 office hours per week. It seems like whenever I do go to office hours, I have to wait in line for the professor to answer my questions. Lines are something you really have to get used to here. Registration is a nightmare because it's really hard to the class schedule you want because classes fill up really quickly. Even though it does take a bit of work and time, you can almost always get the classes you need in some way or another.

## Q Prestigious and Close to Home

I came to UCLA because it is a nationally ranked school. It currently has the biggest history department in the nation, which I am currently studying. It is also far enough for me from home to become independent, yet close enough to be able to go back on weekends.

## The College Prowler Take On...
# Academics

Professors at UCLA are, to say the least, qualified. Many of them hold graduate degrees from prestigious American universities, conduct ground-breaking research, and publish famed books and articles. Due to their class sizes and demanding research schedules, professors don't necessarily beg students to forge relationships. However, almost all hold regular office hours and are happy to reach out once students take the first step. Teaching assistants (TAs), while used widely, are much more sporadic. Some are highly knowledgeable, while others simply do not care about the material, often times making for unfair grading systems. A beacon of hope is that the deeper a student descends into a major, the more attentive professors become, and there are fewer TAs used in the upper-division classes.

Professors and TAs aside, most students agree that the workload at UCLA is manageable as long as procrastination remains the enemy. The quarter system breaks the year into three speedy 10-week chunks, so it's critical to attend lectures and complete work on time. One thing Bruins don't rave about is the course registration process. In a class network barraged by budget cuts, sections fill up quickly, and students' first-choice schedules rarely become realities. However, counselors are present and eager to help students navigate the treacherous course maze, and almost all students are able to fulfill the necessary requirements, even if it means taking that dreaded history seminar.

### The College Prowler® Grade on
### Academics: A-

A high Academics grade generally indicates that professors are knowledgeable, accessible, and genuinely interested in their students' welfare. Other determining factors include class size, how well professors communicate, and whether or not classes are engaging.

# Local Atmosphere

**The Lowdown On...**
## Local Atmosphere

**City, State**
Los Angeles, CA

**Distances to Nearest Major Cities**
San Diego – CA – 2 hours

**Points of Interest**
Bel Air
Beverly Hills
Disneyland
Hollywood
Hollywood Sign
Knott's Berry Farm

Magic Mountain
Malibu and surrounding beaches
Sunset Strip
Universal Studios
Venice Beach

**Shopping Centers**
Third Street Promenade
Westfield Century City
Westside Pavilion

## Major Sports Teams

Anaheim Ducks: NHL
C.D. Chivas USA: Major
League Soccer
Los Angeles Angels of
Anaheim: MLB
Los Angeles Clippers: NBA
Los Angeles Dodgers: MLB
Los Angeles Galaxy: Major
League Soccer
Los Angeles Kings: NHL
Los Angeles Lakers: NBA

## Movie Theaters

**AMC Avco Cinema**
10840 Wilshire Blvd.
Westwood
(310) 475-0711

**Landmark Regent Theater**
1045 Broxton Ave.
Westwood
(310) 281-8223

**Mann Village and Mann
Bruin**
961 Broxton Ave.
Westwood
(310) 208-5576

## Did You Know?

Fun Facts about Los Angeles:

• The Playboy Mansion is about a two-mile run from campus. Students have been known to jog by in search of bunnies.

• Clint Eastwood lives in Bel Air, across the street from the dorms' exit.

• Dozens of movies, from the Twilight saga to George Clooney classics, premier in Westwood each year. Bring your autograph books!

• Westwood was home to the largest concentration of movie theaters. Today, many of the historic theaters still stand, including Fox Theater and Bruin Theater.

• The Janss Investment Company has left its mark all over the Westwood area, from the Janss Steps on UCLA's campus to Westwood Village.

Famous People from L.A.:

- Jennifer Aniston
- Christina Applegate
- Jamie Lee Curtis
- Kate Bosworth
- Leonardo DiCaprio
- Dr. Dre
- Jodie Foster
- Jake and Maggie Gyllenhaal
- Dustin Hoffman
- Kate Hudson
- Angelina Jolie
- Diane Keaton
- Heather Locklear
- Shia LaBeouf
- Marilyn Monroe
- Olson twins
- Gwyneth Paltrow

# Students Speak Out On...
# Local Atmosphere

## Q  City Life
UCLA is in the heart of Los Angeles, minutes away from the Santa Monica Beach.

## Q  Celebrity Sightings If You Pay Attention
Westwood is the best place to go to school because if you stay on your toes, you're likely to see a bunch of celebrities throughout the year.  Movie premieres are always held at the Mann Bruin Theater, about a  three-minute walk from campus. Sometimes movies are filmed around Westwood or on campus, and I've even run into a couple celebs while shopping during a break from class.

## Q  Always Busy
There's alwyas something to see or do in LA. Freshmen pretty much stay in the Westwood bubble, but there are layers of LA waiting to be peeled back as one gets older. When age 21 hits, a whole new world called Sunset Strip opens—the clubs and bars are so much fun!

## Q  Westwood Village
There are awesome movie theaters, shopping, bars, restaurants, tons of fro yo, and public transportation in an upbeat/bustling environment.

## Q  UCLA
There is a lot to do on and outside of the campus. Los Angeles is a very big city with so many things for anyone to do.

## Q Metropolitan, Fun, Big

LA is a crowded city, and UCLA is located in the lively town of Westwood. There are plenty of restaurants and shops, so you will never be bored.

## Q UCLA Fight Fight Fight

Westwood is a few steps away, and you can bus almost anywhere. I mean come on, it's Los Angeles!!

## Q UCLA Rating

UCLA has everything a college campus needs. Within a bus ride, you have the beach, the Grove (with a farmer's market and possible celebrity sightings), malls, boutiques, and concerts. The campus is always abuzz and there is never a dull moment. It's relatively safe because it is in the Westwood area and also because of UCPD. The atmosphere is extremely inviting. I have yet to met a person who wasn't friendly!

# The College Prowler Take On...
# Local Atmosphere

Though many might envision fake breasts and spray tans galore, UCLA's immediate environment is a quaint, funky, and down-to-earth little town. Westwood is a teensy bit of sanity in the midst of wild LA, and all you need to enjoy it is your student ID and a pair of walking shoes. Younger students like to hang out here because of the trendy boutiques, varied cafés, and three movie theaters. Movie stars are often spotted shooting scenes in Westwood's narrow streets or picking up dinner at Whole Foods market, ensuring that LA's buzzing vibe is constantly felt.

With a car, everything changes. Loyola Marymount, Cal State Los Angeles, and the University of Southern California (UCLA's sworn rival) are all within a 20-minute radius. However, although they're close by, students from each university don't usually mingle because of LA's roaring traffic and sections that tend to feel like universe-sized pockets. As for the UCLA galaxy, there are quite a few sights worth checking out that are only a short (cheap) bus or car trip away. LA's clubs are famous in the celebrity world, and there's guaranteed to be an establishment for everyone's interests in town. Legendary theme parks, breathtaking beaches, and historic sites abound, from funky bikes on Venice beach to classy brunches at the Beverly Hilton. The city's jam-packed scale of activities can leave some students feeling overwhelmed, but with a car and some street smarts, Bruins can certainly conquer LA.

**A-**

The College Prowler® Grade on

Local Atmosphere: A-

A high Local Atmosphere grade indicates that the area surrounding campus is safe and scenic. Other factors include nearby attractions, proximity to other schools, and the town's attitude toward students.

# Health & Safety

The Lowdown On...
## Health & Safety

### Security Office
**UCLA Police Department**
Kinross Building, 601
Westwood Plaza
(310) 825-1491
*map.ais.ucla.edu/go/police*

### Safety Services
Anonymous tip line
Blue-light emergency phones
BruinAlert test messaging
system
Crime alerts online
Crime prevention
presentations

Crime reports in The Daily
Bruin
Night campus vans
Night escort services
Rape prevention program
S.T.O.P. Plate Program
(security plates for
electronics)

### Crimes on Campus
Aggravated Assault: 2
Arson: 1
Burglary: 123
Murder/Manslaughter: 0

Robbery: 3
Sex Offenses: 31
Vehicle Theft: 23

## Health Center
### Arthur Ashe Student Health and Wellness Center
221 Westwood Plaza
(310) 825-4073
*www.studenthealth.ucla.edu*
Monday–Thursday 8
a.m.–6:30 p.m., Friday 9
a.m.–6:30 p.m.

## Health Services
Accupuncture
After-hours advice nurse
Allergy shots
Basic medical services
Counseling
Eye care
Immunizations
Massage
Men's health
Occupational therapy
Pharmacy
Physical therapy
Primary care
Psychological services
STD screening
Travel medicine
Tuberculosis screening
Women's health
X-rays

## Day Care Services?
Yes

## Did You Know?

In 1988, Access Control started because homeless people were living in the lounging areas between the north and south side of the dorms. This service kept out the homeless and cut petty theft in the dorms. Campus officials have worked hard to make students feel safe.

### Students Speak Out On...
# Health & Safety

### Q Personal Safety
Being a former fan of USC, the differences in safety are day and night. I do not have to be afraid simply walking to class or being less than 10 feet off campus!

### Q Safety
UCLA is a very safe university. We have our own police department. In addition, we have our very own UCLA EMS service. The campus is extremely well lit, and there are always students on campus. We even have a number you can call to have a UCLA safety van pick you up from anywhere on campus late at night.

### Q UCLA Has Its Own Police Dept. Enough Said.
It's really safe, and I've never felt in danger.

### Q Very Safe
Though the UCLA police aren't very visible on campus, their office does a lot to post where crimes have happened, how to prevent crimes, etc. At orientation, they make the freshmen put the phone number of the UCPD in their phones. Most of campus is very well-lit at night and the police have an escort service back to the dorms.

### Q Amazing Security
UCLA takes various measures to ensure the safety of its students. One example is the Campus Escort Service. If you have a late-night study session at the library and don't feel comfortable walking down the well-lit path to the dorms alone, you can call the Escort Service and a guard will come to walk you right up to the dorm building. There is also a program for people who are out in Westwood late

at night called the Evening Van Service. The van will come pick you up wherever you are within Westwood and drop you back off at the your dorm up throughout the early morning hours. There is also a service to take inebriated students back to their rooms after a night out, and access control in all residence halls after 9 PM.

### Q Safe at All Hours of the Day

It's safe to be on campus late for tutoring or something because there is always someone around, and if you need help walking somewhere there is a number you can call and someone will come and walk you wherever you need to go.

### Q Campus is Like a Neighborhood

The UCLA campus is very safe. It's well lit at night and crawling with on-campus police officers with too much time on their hands. Just today I was confronted by an officer for jaywalking!

### Q Not a Problem

There have been a few little incidents here and there, but for the most part I always feel safe on campus and in the surrounding area, even when I'm alone late at night. I think that really speaks to the niceness of the area and the strength of the university police.

## The College Prowler Take On...
# Health & Safety

Given its big city location, UCLA is a very secure campus by day—the school boasts its own police force and an on-campus record including little more than petty theft. Although campus doesn't feel as safe at night due to its openness and size, UCPD works hard to make Bruins feel assured. Community Service Officers (CSO) are student police who respond to calls for a van ride or walk home from anywhere on campus or in parts of Westwood. Students can simply dial 835-WALK anytime from after dusk until 1 a.m. for an escort, no questions asked.

Once safely at your dorm, you'll encounter Access Control. This team keeps non-residents from trying to enter dorms from 9 p.m. to 5 a.m. Residents must swipe their ID card to enter a dorm during these hours and need to sign in non-resident guests. However, this is not the case in suite-style buildings, which are open to any visitor (or intruder, for that matter) who wishes to enter. Though incidents are rare, the suites are usually the target of on-campus burglaries. While acts of violence or robbery near campus are rare, they are definitely not out of the question in an urban world such as UCLA's. Unlocked off-campus apartments have recently been the target of burglaries, and a smattering of girls have been assaulted while walking solo. However, if caution and care are used, you should feel secure at school.

**B-**

The College Prowler® Grade on
Health & Safety: B-

A high grade in Health & Safety means that students generally feel safe, campus police are visible, blue-light phones and escort services are readily available, and safety precautions are not overly necessary.

# Computers

### The Lowdown On...
## Computers

**Wireless Access**
Yes: Available in certain locations, including Ackerman Union, the library, the lawn, lobbies, and study rooms.

**24-Hour Labs?**
Yes: The library's CLICC lab is open 24 hours during the week before finals and finals week.

**Charged to Print?**
Yes: Students get $5 of free printing each quarter, but after that it's 11 cents per page in the library, and possibly cheaper at other labs.

## Special Software & Hardware Discounts

Hefty discounts are available for students on the following programs: Adobe Acrobat, Adobe Creative Suite, AutoCAD, Corel Painter, Corel Student, FileMaker Pro, Final Cut, Final Draft, iLife, iWork, Mac Box Set, Mac OS X Snow Leopard, Microsoft Office, Microsoft Office, Microsoft Office for Mac, MindManager, MobileMe, Parallels, and VMware Fusion.

## Did You Know?

 The first e-mail message ever was sent from UCLA to Stanford.

## Students Speak Out On...
# Computers

### Q Fast Computers and With Printing Credit for Each Year

The computers closest to me are in Covel Commons, which has more than 20 computers. The computers recently had an upgrade to Windows 7 with faster speed. The best part is that each student is given $5 of printing credit at the start of the school year. There is a small fee for printing after that, but with double-sided printing I can print an entire lecture for less than 20 cents.

### Q Nothing to Complain About

I've never had a problem getting a computer when I've needed it at a lab. The addition of wireless Internet in all the dorms makes doing schoolwork and surfing in general much more convenient. WiFi coverage is solid throughout the campus. No complaints at all.

### Q Computers Are for Everyone!

The entire campus may be accessed through WiF by signing in with a secure log-in. The Internet is fast and reliable. Don't have a computer? Not a problem! Almost all students find a need to use a computer for class work or research, so all of the libraries have desktop computers available for student access (hint: head to less-popular libraries like the Arts Library to avoid 10-minute lines during peak hours). If the computers in the lab you want to work in are filled and you want to skip the wait, laptop computers are almost always available from many of the libraries. They are available for students to rent for four hours at a time. The printers use our Bruin Cards to charge for printing at reasonable prices, less than 10 cents per page. Computer labs will get crowded especially around finals and midterms, so the laptop loans are a great way to circumvent the labs.

### Q Labs Are Always Available

Computer labs at UCLA are always available, especially on the residential hill. This is very convenient. The UCLA library also has laptops available for checkout. Internet speed is fast, but not all locations of the school have wireless.

### Q Review of Computers/Internet at UCLA

There are multiple computer labs with easy access, and students may use them during specific hours for free. There is wireless Internet everywhere with fast speed and very reliable connection.

### Q Labs Are Available When I Need Them

Everyone I know at UCLA has their own computer, so labs are mostly used for the special software that may be necessary for a class. The printers and scanners are also in high demand. WiFi is available throughout campus, with varying strength depending on where you are. Most departments in the school have their own computer labs, and there are also the conveniently placed computer labs in the residential buildings.

### Q Computer Lab

There are new, improved computers than run a lot better than before.

### Q Lots of Computer Labs and Printers

Lots of computers can be found all over campus for student use, and every year you get 100 free pages, and the printers print double sided!

## The College Prowler Take On...
# Computers

At UCLA, computer labs are as plentiful as the California sunshine. Checking e-mail from any of the 17 labs usually requires no more than a five-minute wait. However, finding a computer to use for more than five minutes is slightly more challenging. Students pack the CLICC Lab in the College Library where they can use both Macs and PCs to check e-mail in 10-minute increments or use a computer for schoolwork for up to two hours. However, the line is hefty between classes. The wait for a computer in the main library can take up to 20 minutes at lunchtime, and even then there is a two-hour usage limit. When there is not a class in session, the third floor of Powell is open for student use, and there is hardly ever a line.

The libraries also have electrical outlets and Ethernet hookups scattered around for students looking to study with their own laptops. Or better yet, check one out from the CLICC Lab at Powell Library—this is a little-known secret that will save money and time. Overall, computers at UCLA are plentiful, but the labs still lack the freedom to snag an A grade. One plus, however, is the network's incredible speed and reliability. With three new networks recently added to the mix, it's a snap to find a good connection on campus.

**B**

The College Prowler® Grade on

Computers: B

A high grade in Computers designates that computer labs are available, the computer network is easily accessible, and the campus's computing technology is up-to-date.

# Facilities

**The Lowdown On...**
## Facilities

**Campus Size**
419 acres

**Student Centers**
Ackerman Union
North Campus Student
Center

**Main Libraries**
Powell Library

**Service & Maintenance Staff**
1,341

**Popular Places to Chill**
Ackerman Union
Bruin Café
The hill near Janss Steps
Northern Lights
Sunset Canyon Recreation
Center

## Bar on Campus

None

## Bowling on Campus

None

## Coffeehouse on Campus

Jimmy's Coffee House in Lu Valle Commons
Kerckhoff Coffeehouse in Kerckhoff Hall
Northern Lights in the North Campus Student Center

## Movie Theater on Campus

The James Bridges Theater in Melnitz Hall

## Favorite Things To Do

Between classes, students like to soak up sun, grab some
chow, sculpt a stellar body at the gym, or play a round of pool.
The pre-screenings at UCLA are always packed, regardless
of how a movie is going to do at the box office. There are
also events, from speakers to plays, at the North Campus
Auditorium each week. At the end of the year, students like to
check out cultural shows—there is a show every day from 12
p.m. to 1 p.m. in Ackerman Square, but the end of the year is
best because the squads have gotten in a lot practice.

## "Green" Initiatives

UCLA joined the "green" bandwagon years ago, when the
University began recycling 44 percent of its waste via the
Facilities Management Recycling Program. Students are
encouraged to recycle in the dorms, and pilot programs are
being conducted that instate compost-making programs in
some buildings. Housing is also skilled at coming up with
incentives that motivate residents to conserve power.

## Did You Know?

In addition to UCLA's main library—Powell—there are 11 other libraries: Arts, Biomedical, Clark Memorial, College, East Asian, Management, Music, Performing Arts, Research, Science and Engineering, and UCLA Lab School libraries. This doesn't include all the special collections and reading rooms also available.

While there isn't a bowling alley on campus now, there used to be one in Ackerman about 20 years ago!

## Students Speak Out On...
# Facilities

### Q Ackerman Union-Bookstore
The student bookstore is THE place to go for anything UCLA-related. Clothing, sports stuff, etc., all can be found here. The atmosphere is great. The layout is wonderful. What more can you ask for?

### Q Amazing Campus and Facilities
The University of California - Los Angeles has the most amazing campus I have seen in California, or any other state. There are many libraries to choose from, but my personal favorite is Powell Library. It has many quiet places to study and many places to study in groups. The lecture halls are amazing as well, equipped with microphones, projectors, and such.

### Q Best Facilities!!!
The facilities at UCLA are absolutely fantastic. We have the best gym of any other school I have been to, and it includes a rock-climbing wall, cardio machines, weights, more fitness classes than you could ever think of attending, and great volleyball and basketball courts. We also have state-of-the-art athletic facilities that all students have a chance to use through IM or club sports. The 17 libraries on campus give more than enough room for any studying you need to do, too!

### Q Architectural Diversity
The architecture at UCLA is amazing. It is varied so everyone will find something that pleases their eye. The main campus has an Ivy League feel with brick buildings

and stained glass windows. On the flip side, the new art department is in a beautiful modern building with views out of all the glass windows.

## Q Libraries

The libraries are wonderful. There are lots of books, places to read and study, and most of all, they are very close to the vending machines where you will find the most amazing vanilla coffee on the planet.

## Q Beautiful Architecture and Landscape

The feel of the UCLA campus is lush and beautiful. You are surrounded by a lot greenery and excellent brickwork and architecture. Daily walks through the campus are always breathtaking. The student union has beautiful archways on the outside and modern design on the inside. Our student gym is top of the line. The student union is filled with fast food restaurants, a student store, and anything you need.

## Q A World Class University- With World Class Facilities

UCLA has amazing, picture-perfect facilities that attest to its reputation of being world-class. There is the enormous yet cozy ornate Powell Library; Royce Hall within the same breathtaking court, where you can enjoy music, theater, and other performance for student prices; John Wooden Center, a large gym located in the heart of campus in Bruin Plaza that offers a variety of high caliber workout equipment; and Ackerman Union, a multi-story facility where you can get fast food, buy textbooks, and stop by the enormous UCLA store all in one go! Besides the obvious ones, there is also Kerkchoff, the distinctly Hogwarts-like building that contains a coffee house, study room, and a Grand Salon where one can catch student-produced standup comedy or open mic sessions; a planetarium atop the Math and Science Building complete with enormous telescopes that are free and open to the public; several multi-story research libraries where one can really get some studying done; and a modern Student

Activities Building where you can find out how to get involved in some of the student clubs and visit the Testing Bank to practice for an upcoming exam. That's just the main section of campus and just a few facilities!

## Q Pretty Nice

For all of the bad things I could say about UCLA, I have no complaints about the campus. There are several libraries available, some of which are under renovation, but the main library is beautiful and very useful. There is a gym open to all students from early in the morning through the late night, equipped with racquetball courts, a rock wall, basketball courts, a weight room, and cardio equipment.

# The College Prowler Take On...
# Facilities

UCLA's athletic pride is evident when looking at most facilities. The track is gorgeous, the fields are spacious, and John Wooden Center is beautiful. Wooden, the gym where non-varsity Bruins exercise, is an athlete's dream with an extensive weight room, three basketball courts, two volleyball courts, tons of racquetball courts, a rock-climbing wall, cardio equipment galore, and private rooms offering lessons in everything from karate to salsa dancing. With a locker room and sauna, Wooden attracts A-listers like Magic Johnson and Adam Sandler, who have been known to play pick-up with star-struck students. UCLA's marina is a 25-minute drive from campus and offers competitively priced instruction in sports like scuba and rowing.

But, however nice many facilities are, UC could easily stand for Under Construction. Pauley Pavilion's re-doing is about to get underway, and messy building renovations seem like a regular part of campus life. One thing that hasn't changed in awhile, however, is the gorgeous Powell Library. A hotspot for brainiac Bruins, Powell's cushy couches, plentiful outlets, and vaulted ceilings are a highlight of the studying experience. Nearly a dozen other libraries on campus offer similar satisfaction.

**B+**

### The College Prowler® Grade on
### Facilities: B+

A high Facilities grade indicates that the campus is aesthetically pleasing and well-maintained; facilities are state-of-the-art, and libraries are exceptional. Other determining factors include the quality of both athletic and student centers and an abundance of things to do on campus.

# Campus Dining

The Lowdown On...
## Campus Dining

**Meal Plan Available?**
Yes

**Average Meals/Week**
19

**Freshman Meal Plan Required?**
Yes: All on-campus resident students get a meal plan.

**24-Hour Dining**
None

# Dining Halls & Campus Restaurants

**Bruin Café**
Location: Bottom floor of Sproul Hall
Food: Coffee, pastries, sandwiches, salads
Hours: Monday–Friday 7 a.m.–2 a.m., Saturday–Sunday 3 p.m.–2 a.m.

**Café 1919**
Location: Covel Commons
Food: Frozen yogurt, gelato, paninis, pizza, salads
Hours: Monday–Friday 8:30 a.m.–10 a.m., 11:30 a.m.–3 p.m., 5 p.m.–12 a.m.

**Café Synapse**
Location: Gonda Center
Food: Pasta, pizza, sandwiches, specialty drinks
Hours: Monday–Thursday 7 a.m.–5 p.m., Friday 7:30 a.m.–4:30 p.m.

**Carl's Jr.**
Location: Cooperage ("the Coop"), Ackerman Union
Food: Burgers
Hours: Monday–Friday 7 a.m.–9 p.m., Saturday–Sunday 8:30 a.m.–4 p.m.

**Covel Commons Residential Restaurant**
Location: Covel Commons
Food: All-you-can-eat breakfast, grill, pasta, pizza, salad/soup bar
Hours: Monday–Friday 7 a.m.–9 a.m., 11 a.m.–2 p.m., 5 p.m.–9 p.m., Saturday–Sunday 11:30 a.m.–3 p.m., 5 p.m.–9 p.m.

**Curbside**
Location: Cooperage ("the Coop"), Ackerman Union
Food: Convenience store
Hours: Monday–Thursday 10 a.m.–9 p.m., Friday 10 a.m.–7 p.m.

**De Neve Residential Restaurant**
Location: De Neve Plaza
Food: All-you-can-eat breakfast; bagel/salad/soup bar; European grill; international dishes; late-night burgers; fries, shakes, and pizza; make-your-own sandwiches
Hours: Monday–Friday 7 a.m.–10 a.m., 11 a.m.–2 p.m., 5 p.m.–8 p.m., 9 p.m.–12 a.m., Saturday–Sunday 9:30 a.m.–2 p.m., 5 p.m.–8 p.m., 9 p.m.–12 a.m.

**Espresso Roma Café**
Location: Anderson School of Business
Food: Salads, sandwiches
Hours: Monday–Thursday 7 a.m.–9 p.m., Friday 7 a.m.–7 p.m., Saturday 9 a.m.–7 p.m., Sunday 10 a.m.–9 p.m.

## Greenhouse

Location: Terrace Food Court, Ackerman Union
Food: Healthy
Hours: Monday–Thursday 7 a.m.–7 p.m., Friday 7 a.m.–5 p.m.

## Hedrick Residential Restaurant

Location: Hedrick Hall
Food: All-you-can-eat sushi, grill, make-your-own stir-fry, organic salad/soup bar
Hours: Monday–Friday 11 a.m.–2 p.m., 5 p.m.–8 p.m., Saturday–Sunday 9:30 a.m.–2 p.m., 5 p.m.–8 p.m.

## Jamba Juice

Location: Cooperage ("the Coop"), Ackerman Union
Food: Smoothies
Hours: Monday–Friday 7 a.m.–7 p.m., Saturday–Sunday 11 a.m.–4 p.m.

## Jimmy's Coffee House

Location: Lu Valle Commons
Food: Baked goods, coffee
Hours: Monday–Thursday 7 a.m.–9 p.m., Friday 7 a.m.–6 p.m., Saturday–Sunday 8 a.m.–5 p.m.

## Kerckhoff Coffee House

Location: Kerckhoff Hall
Food: Baskin Robbins, Good For You (vegetarian), Grab & Go Gourmet, Kikka Sushi

Hours: Monday–Thursday 8 a.m.–11 p.m., Friday 7 a.m.–7 p.m., Saturday–Sunday 8 a.m.–6 p.m.

## Lu Valle Commons

Location: Near School of Law
Food: California Toss (pizza and salad), Honorable Subs, Pacific Rice & Noodle Traders, Roadside Grill
Hours: Monday–Thursday 7:30 a.m.–9 p.m., Friday 7:30 a.m.–4 p.m., Saturday 11 a.m.–3 p.m.

## North Campus Student Center

Location: Near Young Research Library
Food: Burger Express, California Café (pizza, entrees), Casa Norte (Mexican), Grab & Go Gourmet, Stacks Deli
Hours: Monday–Thursday 7 a.m.–7:30 p.m., Friday 7 a.m.–7 p.m.

## Northern Lights

Location: North of Rolfe Hall
Food: Baskin Robbins, Kikka Sushi
Hours: Monday–Thursday 7 a.m.–7:30 p.m., Friday 7 a.m.–7 p.m.

## Panda Express

Location: Terrace Food Court, Ackerman Union
Food: Chinese

Hours: Monday–Thursday 10 a.m.–9 p.m., Friday 10 a.m.–8 p.m., Saturday 11 a.m.–6 p.m., Sunday 11 a.m.–4 p.m.

## Relaxation

Location: Terrace Food Court, Ackerman Union
Food: Boba tea
Hours: Monday–Thursday 9 a.m.–7:30 p.m., Friday 9 a.m.–6 p.m., Saturday 11 a.m.–5 p.m., Sunday 11 a.m.–4 p.m.

## Rendezvous

Location: Rieber Terrace
Food: Asian, Mexican
Hours: Monday–Friday 7:30 a.m.–11 a.m., 12 p.m.–5 p.m., 6 p.m.–12 a.m.

## Rieber Residential Restaurant

Location: Rieber Hall
Food: American, international
Hours: Monday–Thursday 11 a.m.–2 p.m., 5 p.m.–8 p.m., Sunday 10:30 a.m.–2 p.m., 5 p.m.–8 p.m.

## Rubio's

Location: Terrace Food Court, Ackerman Union
Food: Mexican
Hours: Monday–Thursday 10 a.m.–9 p.m., Friday 10 a.m.–8 p.m., Saturday 11 a.m.–6 p.m., Sunday 11 a.m.–3 p.m.

## Rx

Location: Terrace Food Court, Ackerman Union
Food: Candy
Hours: Monday–Thursday 9 a.m.–8 p.m., Friday 9 a.m.–6 p.m., Saturday 11 a.m.–5 p.m., Sunday 11 a.m.–4 p.m.

## Sbarro

Location: Terrace Food Court, Ackerman Union
Food: Italian
Hours: Monday–Thursday 10 a.m.–9 p.m., Friday 10 a.m.–8 p.m., Saturday 11 a.m.–6 p.m., Sunday 11 a.m.–3 p.m.

## Taco Bell

Location: Cooperage ("the Coop"), Ackerman Union
Food: Mexican
Hours: Monday–Friday 9:30 a.m.–9 p.m.

## Tsunami

Location: Ackerman Union
Food: Asian
Hours: Monday–Thursday 10 a.m.–7 p.m., Friday 10 a.m.–5 p.m.

## Wetzel's Pretzels

Location: Terrace Food Court, Ackerman Union
Food: Pretzels
Hours: Monday–Thursday 9 a.m.–8 p.m., Friday 9 a.m.–6 p.m., Saturday 11 a.m.–5 p.m., Sunday 11 a.m.–4 p.m.

## Student Favorites: Campus Dining Hall

De Neve Residential Restaurant

## Student Favorites: Campus Restaurant/ Vendor

Carl's Jr. in Ackerman Union

## Student Favorites: Breakfast Food on Campus

Oatmeal, fruit, and bagel sandwiches from Rendezvous

## Student Favorites: Lunch/Dinner Entrée on Campus

Paninis and pizza from Café 1919

## Student Favorites: Late-night Snack on Campus

Bread bowls and muffins from Bruin Café

## Off-Campus Places to Use Flex Money

Acapulco Mexican Restaurant y Cantina
Baja Fresh Mexican Grill
Baskin-Robbins
BJ's Pizza
Burger King
Chipotle

Denny's
Jerry's Famous Deli
Pastagina
Red Mango
Rocky Mountain Chocolate Factory
Sepi's Giant Submarines
Tengu
Trimana
Whole Foods

## Special Options

Each residential dining facility provides tasty vegetarian and vegan options, but the on-campus vendors and cafés don't make the same effort.

Two food trucks offers everything from tacos to skewers in the Court of Sciences on weekdays.

## Did You Know?

There is a sack-lunch program that allows dorm residents to swap a dorm lunch for a sack lunch, which includes a sandwich, fruit pack, and chips.

## Students Speak Out On...
# Campus Dining

### Q UCLA Dining
UCLA offers a wide variety of food options to its students. Each of the four dormitory dining halls offers a fresh and diverse menu that is open to both students and non-students. Along with the dining halls, several eateries are scattered around the dorms, as well as all over campus, and provide anything from quick burgers to Asian to loaded gourmet salad bars. The student union, known as Ackerman, is a wonderful location that houses a small market along with the fast food/snack stations.

### Q Excellent Dining Quality and Options
There is tons of variety. We have multiple ethnic foods ranging from Mexican burritos and quesadillas; Chinese orange chicken and varieties of fried rice; Thai and Indian curry; Italian-style pizzas, pastas, and paninis; and your standard hamburgers, sandwiches, and wraps.

### Q Food Is Great
It's ranked second in the nation, so the food at UCLA is terrific. They always mix it up so you don't get bored, and it always tastes great. You'll find everything from pizza to burgers to rice dishes and pasta. There are also a lot of pastries and ice cream for dessert.

### Q The Great Advantage of Eating on Campus
The food around campus is excellent, I can literally eat there all week, and have breakfast, lunch and dinner there. The food is delicious and healthy.

## Q Yum!

Dining on campus is better than my mom's kitchen! Every dining hall has a theme or "specialty"—they're all delicious. Hedrick Hall even has sushi twice a week.

## Q So Good

Our dining halls are seriously some of the best in the nation. Sushi, make-your-own stir-fry, paninis, bread bowls, Coffee Bean drinks, and the best muffins ever are all over the place at UCLA.

## Q Food and Variety Are Amazing

UCLA dining is rated one of the best in the country, and it definitely shows. Each of the dining halls that are buffet-style offers a wide arrangement of meals every night— rarely will nothing appeal to you. Bruin Café is open until 2 a.m. and is a common gathering spot late Thursday and Friday nights. 14 Premier is the best meal plan to get as a freshman, unless you're a student athlete or have a large appetite.

## Q UCLA Dining: Lots of Choices!

The food here is really fantastic. It's annoying sometimes that the dining halls are closed from 3 to 5 p.m., but residential restaurants are open at those times, and they are great. Chinese, Mexican, and typical American (sandwiches, salads, bagels, smoothies, etc.) are available to spice up the dining hall selection. Options aren't as great on weekends, but there is still almost always SOMETHING open on campus.

### The College Prowler Take On...
# Campus Dining

Food at UCLA is delicious. Each "residential restaurant" revolves its choices around a tasty central theme, such as American comfort foods or Asian and organic. These restaurants switch up their menus constantly to include creative favorites like penne with shrimp or chicken cordon bleu burgers. Although bad-for-you temptations abound, there's no shortage of healthy, vegetarian, and vegan options—each restaurant features a colorful salad bar and plenty of veggie-based entrees. The dorm zone has three quick-service restaurants, each of which is a welcome break when dining hall food becomes (if ever!) monotonous. Mean plan options are well-priced and range from 11 to 19 meals a week, though most students agree that the flexible 14 Premier plan is the way to go, as it allows unused meal "swipes" to carry over from day to day.

Outside the Hill, non-residential food offerings are almost just as fabulous. Ackerman Union hosts a variety of popular vendors and equally satisfying prices, including the largest Jamba Juice in the nation. Campus cafés, such as Northern Lights and Jimmy's Coffee House, provide an upperclassman's escape from the school day and a cozy place to study or chat.

**A-**

**The College Prowler® Grade on**

Campus Dining: A-

The grade on Campus Dining addresses the quality of both school-owned dining halls and independent on-campus restaurants as well as the price, availability, and variety of food.

# Off-Campus Dining

**The Lowdown On...**
## Off-Campus Dining

### Restaurant Listings

**Acapulco Mexican Restaurant y Cantina**
Food: Mexican
1109 Glendon Ave.
(310) 208-3884
*www.acapulcorestaurants.com*
Price: $5–$10
Cool Features: Free buffet-style appetizers and half-priced meals on Monday nights.

**Baja Fresh**
Food: Mexican
10916 Lindbrook Dr., Westwood
(310) 208-3317
*www.bajafresh.com*
Price: $5–$10

**BJ's Restaurant & Brewhouse**
Food: American
939 Broxton Ave., Westwood
(310) 209-7475
*www.bjsbrewhouse.com*
Price: $5–$10

### California Pizza Kitchen

Food: Pizza
1001 Broxton Ave.,
Westwood
(310) 209-9197
*www.cpk.com*
Price: $10–$15
Cool Features: CPK has more
than 30 different types of
pizza.

### Canter's Delicatessen and Restaurant

Food: Deli
419 N. Fairfax Ave.
(323) 651-2030
*www.cantersdeli.com*
Price: $5–$10
Cool Features: Authentic
East Coast diner on the West
Coast.

### Corner Bakery Café

Food: Baked goods,
sandwiches, soup
1019 Westwood Blvd.,
Westwood
(310) 824-1314
*www.cornerbakery.com*
Price: $5–$12

### Damon & Pythias Food for the Gods

Food: American
1061 Broxton Ave.,
Westwood
(310) 824-8777
Price: $8–$15

### Diddy Riese

Food: Cookies
926 Broxton Ave., Westwood
(310) 208-0448
*www.diddyriese.com*
Price: $1–$5
Cool Features: A giant cookie
and ice cream sandwich costs
$1.50.

### Enzo's Pizzeria

Food: Italian, pizza
10940 Weyburn Ave.,
Westwood
(310) 208-3696
Price: $5–$10

### Espresso Profeta

Food: Baked goods, coffee
1129 Glendon Ave.,
Westwood
(310) 208-3375
Price: $5–$10

### Gushi

Food: Korean
978 Gayley Ave., Westwood
(310) 208-4038
*www.ilovegushi.com*
Price: $5–$10

### Headlines Diner & Press Club

Food: American, diner
10922 Kinross Ave.,
Westwood
(310) 208-2424
*www.headlinesdiner.com*
Price: $5–$10

### In-N-Out Burger
Food: Fast food
922 Gayley Ave., Westwood
(310) 208-2821
*www.in-n-out.com*
Price: $2–$5

### Italian Express
Food: Italian, pizza
10845 Lindbrook Dr.,
Westwood
(310) 208-5572
Price: $5–$10

### Jerry's Famous Deli
Food: Deli
10925 Weyburn Ave.,
Westwood
(310) 208-3354
*www.jerrysfamousdeli.com*
Price: $5–$10
Cool Features: This is one of
the most popular restaurants
in Los Angeles.

### Lamonica's New York Pizza
Food: Pizza
1066 Gayley Ave., Westwood
(310) 208-8671
*www.lamonicasnypizza.com*
Price: $5–$10
Cool Features: Classic New
York thin-crust pizza.

### Mel's Drive-In Restaurant
Food: American
1650 N. Highland Ave.,
Hollywood
(323) 465-3111
*www.melsdrive-in.com*
Price: $5–$10

Cool Features: This classic
50's-style drive-in diner
was featured in the movie
"American Grafitti."

### Napa Valley Grille
Food: California cuisine
1100 Glendon Ave.,
Westwood
(310) 824-3322
*www.napavalleygrille.com*
Price: $20–50

### Noodle Planet
Food: Asian noodles
1118 Westwood Blvd.
(310) 208-0777
*www.thai-food.com/
noodleplanet*
Price: $5–$10

### Novel Café
Food: Breakfast, coffee,
desserts, sandwiches
1101 Gayley Ave., Westwood
(310) 208-6410
*www.novelcafe.com*
Price: $5–$12

### Sak's Teriyaki
Food: Japanese
1121 Glendon Ave.,
Westwood
(310) 208-2002
Price: $5–$10

### Tommy Taco (aka "Buck Fiddy's")
Food: Mexican
954 Gayley Ave., Westwood
(310) 824-4114
Price: $1–$5

**Tomodachi Sushi**
Food: Sushi
10975 Weyburn Ave.,
Westwood
(310) 824-8805
Price: $7–$20

**Versailles**
Food: Cuban
10319 Venice Blvd.
(310) 558-3168
*www.versaillescuban.com*
Price: $8–$15

**Yamato**
Food: Japanese
1099 Westwood Blvd.,
Westwood
(310) 208-0100
*www.yamatorestaurants.com*
Price: $10–$15

**Yogurtland**
Food: Frozen yogurt
10911 Lindbrook Dr.,
Westwood
(310) 208-2888
*www.yogurt-land.com*
Price: $3–$6

## Best Asian

Tomodachi Sushi

## Best Breakfast

Corner Bakery Café
Headlines Diner & Press Club

## Best Coffee

Corner Bakery Café
Espresso Profeta

## Best Dessert

BJ's Restaurant & Brewhouse
Diddy Riese
Yogurtland

## Best Healthy

Baja Fresh
Damon & Pythias Food for
the Gods

## Best Late-Night

In-N-Out Burger
Italian Express
Tommy Taco

## Best Mexican

Acapulco Mexican Restaurant
y Cantina

## Best Pizza

Enzo's Pizzeria
Italian Express

## Best Place to Take a Date

Novel Cafe
Yamato

## Best Place to Take Your Parents

California Pizza Kitchen
Napa Valley Grille

## 24-Hour Dining

Canter's Delicatessen and
Restaurant
Mel's Drive-In Restaurant

## Other Places to Check Out

Gypsy Café
Habibi Café
Le Chine Wok
Subway
Thai House
Togo's Eatery
Westwood Brewing Company

## Grocery Stores

**Ralphs**
10861 Wayburn Ave.,
Westwood
(310) 824-5994
*ralphs.com*
Daily 24 hours

**Trader Joe's**
1000 Glendon Ave.
(310) 824-1495
*www.traderjoes.com*
Daily 8 a.m.–10 p.m.

**Whole Foods Market**
1050 Gayley Ave.
(310) 824-0858
*wholefoodsmarket.com*
Daily 7 a.m.–10 p.m.

## Did You Know?

Acapulco has free buffet-style appetizers and half-priced meals on Monday nights.

## Students Speak Out On...
# Off-Campus Dining

### Q Convenient Close, and Affordable
There are a lot of nearby restaurants and supermarkets.

### Q Good to GO
I would definitely say Westwood Village is a good place to chill out. You can find any kind of food you want. It has so many different varieties and all are within a mile distant of the school.

### Q The Best
Los Angeles has a great variety of places to eat out. There are many places with high-quality cusine, and some local eateries known for unique menus.

### Q Westwood Eateries.
UCLA lies in the heart of Westwood—a borough of West Los Angeles. It's a  quaint little college village with lots of privately owned Asian and Italian restaurants. There is more variety and it is all very comfortable for a student's price range. Most places offer a percentage discount with the presentation of a UCLA student ID.

### Q Great Off-Campus Eateries
UCLA has tons of great off-campus eateries, including great fast food such as In-N-Out and Taco Bell to more upscale restaurant like BJs Brewery. Dennys has a 10 percent off student discount. All of these locations are close to campus, just a 5- to 10-minute walk away, and the atmosphere is amazing!

## ℚ So Good

I love the sushi in L.A.—it's a really trendy thing. We are in a huge city, so there's a restaurant for everyone. There's upscale Italian and good old McDonald's, so I've never been disappointed by this city.

## ℚ Whole Foods

Cost is average. There is a great variety of food choices, and the food is healthy. Already prepared meals taste like homemade.

## ℚ Cheap and Yummy

There are a million sushi and frozen yogurt places in Westwood, and lots of them allow you to pay with your student ID card. Students also are offered discounts or specials frequently.

# The College Prowler Take On...
# Off-Campus Dining

For students with a little more determination and a tad pudgier wallet, off-campus dining is a common adventure—and it is certainly a good one. There are plenty of options near UCLA's campus in Westwood. For lunch, healthy and cheap sandwiches can be found at Corner Bakery Café, Damon and Pythias, or Socko's. Subs around here are filling and often named after Bruin greats, such as John Wooden, Bill Walton, and Kareem Abdul-Jabbar. For an after-class treat, try In-N-Out Burger or a little cup of topping-sprinkled heaven at Yogurtland. Dinner is always delicious at BJ's Restaurant & Brewhouse or one of Westwood's seemingly endless sushi options.

If you want to venture farther from campus, the area surrounding Westwood is home to scores of taste-bud playgrounds, from alley dives to Sunset bars owned by Ashton Kutcher. Just like its people, Los Angeles's food scene is diverse and amazing, so while at UCLA, make sure to take advantage of the plethora of food options around you. It will be an educational and culinary experience that your stomach will surely thank you for!

**The College Prowler® Grade on**

**Off-Campus Dining: A**

A high Off-Campus Dining grade implies that off-campus restaurants are affordable, accessible, and worth visiting. Other factors include the variety of cuisine and the availability of alternative options (vegetarian, vegan, kosher).

# Campus Housing

**The Lowdown On...**
## Campus Housing

**On-Campus Housing Available?**
Yes

**Campus Housing Capacity**
13,249

**Number of Dormitories**
13

**Number of Campus-Owned Apartments**
7

## Dormitories

### De Neve Plaza
Floors: 4
Number of Occupants: 1,000+
Bathrooms: Private
Coed: Yes
Residents: Freshmen, sophomores, juniors
Room Types: Doubles, triples
Special Features: Air conditioning, central courtyard, computer labs, fitness room, laundry facilities, residential restaurant, study lounges.

### Dykstra Hall
Floors: 10
Number of Occupants: 750–999
Bathrooms: Communal
Coed: Yes
Residents: Freshmen, sophomores, juniors
Room Types: Doubles, triples
Special Features: Floor lounges, laundry facilities, TV lounges.

### Hedrick Hall
Floors: 7
Number of Occupants: 1,000+
Bathrooms: Communal
Coed: Yes
Residents: Mostly freshmen
Room Types: Doubles, triples
Special Features: Computer lab, dining hall, fitness room, music practice room, ping-pong and pool tables, private study rooms, study lounge.

### Hedrick Summit
Floors: 9
Number of Occupants: 750–999
Bathrooms: Private
Coed: Yes
Residents: Freshmen, sophomores, juniors
Room Types: Singles, doubles, triples
Special Features: Floor lounges, laundry facilities, rec room, TV lounge.

### Hitch Suites
Floors: 3
Number of Occupants: 250–499
Bathrooms: Suite-style
Coed: Yes
Residents: Mostly freshmen and sophomores
Room Types: Two-bedroom suites
Special Features: Each suite has living room and private entries. Complex has conference rooms, laundry facilities, sundeck.

### Rieber Hall
Floors: 7
Number of Occupants: 750–999
Bathrooms: Communal
Coed: Yes
Residents: Mostly freshmen

Room Types: Doubles, triples
Special Features: Computer lab, conference room, dining hall, fitness room, floor lounges, large-screen TV, music practice room, ping-pong and pool tables, study lounge.

### Rieber Terrace

Floors: 9
Number of Occupants: 500–749
Bathrooms: Some private, some shared
Coed: Yes
Residents: Freshmen, upperclassmen
Room Types: Doubles, triples, suites
Special Features: Floor lounges, laundry facilities, meeting room, Rendezvous restaurant, study space.

### Rieber Vista

Floors: 9
Number of Occupants: 500–749
Bathrooms: Private or suite-style
Coed: Yes
Residents: Freshmen, sophomores, juniors
Room Types: Singles, doubles, triples
Special Features: Computer labs, dining hall, fitness rooms, laundry facilities, music practice rooms, study lounges.

### Saxon Suites

Floors: 3
Number of Occupants: 250–499
Bathrooms: Suite-style
Coed: Yes
Residents: Mostly sophomores and juniors
Room Types: Two-bedroom suites
Special Features: Each suite has living room and private entries. Complex has conference room, sand volleyball court.

### Sproul Hall

Floors: 7
Number of Occupants: 1,000+
Bathrooms: Communal
Coed: Yes
Residents: Freshmen, sophomores, juniors
Room Types: Doubles, triples
Special Features: Computer lab, conference room, fitness room, floor lounges, music practice room, ping-pong and pool tables, study lounge, TV lounge.

### Sunset Village: Canyon Point

Floors: 4
Number of Occupants: 500–749
Bathrooms: Private
Coed: Yes
Residents: Freshmen, sophomores, juniors

Room Types: Doubles, triples
Special Features: Air
conditioning and eight study
lounges. Building commons
has computer lab, restaurant,
and study space.

### Sunset Village: Courtside

Floors: 4
Number of Occupants:
500–749
Bathrooms: Private
Coed: Yes
Residents: Freshmen,
sophomores, juniors
Room Types: Doubles, triples
Special Features: Individual
climate control for each
room, elevators, laundry
facilities, and a study lounge.
Building commons has
computer lab, restaurant, and
study space.

### Sunset Village: Delta Terrace

Floors: 4
Number of Occupants:
250–499
Bathrooms: Private
Coed: Yes
Residents: Freshmen,
sophomores, juniors
Room Types: Doubles, triples
Special Features: Barbecue
grill, eight study lounges,
laundry facilities, picnic
patio. Building commons has
computer lab, restaurant, and
study space.

## Campus-Owned Apartments

### North Campus Apartments

Number of Units: 250+
Bathrooms: Private
Coed: Yes
Residents: Upperclassmen
Room Types: Studio, one-,
two-, and three-bedroom
apartments
These complexes are closer
to campus and dining halls
than some dorms, making
them a great pick for
independent underclassmen
or those hoping to maintain
that younger-student vibe.
Special Features: The
undergraduate apartments
are spread out over seven
complexes: Glenrock,
Glenrock West, Gayley
Towers, Landfair, Margan,
Westwood Chateau, and
Westwood Palm. Units are
furnished and complexes
have laundry facilities.

# Freshmen Living On Campus

94%

# Undergrads Living On Campus

36%

# Best Freshman Dorms

De Neve Plaza
Hedrick Summit

# Best Upperclassman Dorms

Hitch Suites
Saxon Suites
Sproul Hall

# Worst Freshman Dorms

Dykstra Hall
Hedrick Hall

# Worst Upperclassman Dorms

Dykstra Hall
Hedrick Hall

# Types of Housing Offered

Apartments for married
students
Apartments for single
students
Coed dorms
Cooperative housing
Fraternity/sorority housing
Special housing for disabled
students
Theme housing
Wellness housing

# What You Get

Bed
Cable TV and access to
UCLA TV
Closet
Desk and chair
Phone

# Available for Rent

MicroFridges can be rented
and vacuum cleaners can be
borrowed from RAs.

# Also Available

Sproul Hall offers theme
communities, such as the
Chicano/a Floor and the
Sustainability Floor, and there
are plans for integrating more
theme communities into the
residence halls. Single rooms
are hard to come by, but they
do exist, as well.

There are University
apartments for grad students,
as well as married students,
same-sex domestic partners,
and single parents.

## Students Speak Out On...
# Campus Housing

### Q Love My Roomies!
When applying for campus housing, the coordiators take into consideration the similarities and interests of the roommates. I have made lifelong friends with my college roommates simply because of the superb matching of interests.

### Q UCLA Living
Despite the cost of living in the dorms at UCLA, it is definitely an experience worth having. The accommodations that UCLA has to offer are not only state-of-the-art, but they are essential to the UCLA experience. With the opportunity to socialize and bond with your fellow Bruins in a comfortable and secure place, the UCLA students thrives in such a community.

### Q Residence Halls
Living on campus in a residence hall is awesome, especially as a freshman. The residence halls are extremely social and always a good time. Having an on-campus meal plan is a must at UCLA. We have, by far, the best food out of any campus I've heard of.

### Q Social Atmoshphere
Housing is adequate, as long as you're not expecting the Ritz. It's as best as can be expected.

### Q Living on the Hill Is a Great First-Year Experience
Living on "the Hill" (where all the dorms are) is the only way to go as a freshman. Because everyone's concentrated in one place, it's easy to get around to each other, and there are lots of spaces to study/eat/hangout. The suites

are a popular place to pre-game before going out, and they're really fun. Most RAs are really friendly and laid-back. Most people live on campus for their first two years and move off campus for the last two.

## Q Residence Halls

I lived in Sproul Hall my first year, and it was great. Unlike suites or plazas, halls have laundry machines on every floor. Halls are also great for socializing because people are always moving around in the hallways. If you leave your door open, someone is bound to pop in and say hi. The only downside is that the rooms themselves are smaller than rooms in other buildings, but you hardly spend any time in your room anyway.

## Q Res Halls are Cramped but Have a Great Social Atmosphere

While most upperclassmen choose to live off campus, freshmen and sophomores have the choice between brand-new plazas and suites or older residence halls. Though the plazas and suites are more spacious and modern, there is no better way to instantly meet people than life in a res hall.

## Q Hall Life Is a Lot More Social

I moved from a private plaza into a hall midway through my second quarter, and it was a great decision. My old plaza was very anti-social and people didn't get along as well as they do in a residence hall.

# The College Prowler Take On...
# Campus Housing

On UCLA's "Hill," students can opt for one of two scenarios: enjoying the sardine lifestyle while making friends with fellow sardines, or savoring a spacious existence while meeting virtually nobody. The residence halls are undergoing a renovation process, which means some are brand-new while others are horrendously outdated and ridiculously over-inhabited (but are on the list to be renovated). Whatever the case, these halls offer the quintessential freshman dorm experience—floor-wide hangout sessions are the norm and lifelong friends are made often. Freshmen bond over complaints of crowding and communal bathrooms, making for an experience that's almost a rite of passage at UCLA. On the flip side, suite buildings and complexes deliver the promises their higher price tags bring. These options offer more serene lifestyles, with private bathrooms in all units and living rooms with a table and couch in some, but due to the apartment-like nature of these choices, social interaction is scarce.

Regardless of the housing system's shortcomings, students do enjoy living at UCLA and can typically find something to suit their lifestyle preference. All dorms, no matter how crowded, are clean and sanitary with some form of lounge, and dining halls are very close by. In about half of the buildings, wireless Internet access is available in individual rooms, while the rest feature reliable wireless in the lounges.

**B**

### The College Prowler® Grade on

Campus
Housing: B

A high Campus Housing grade indicates that dorms are clean, well-maintained, and spacious. Other determining factors include variety of dorms, proximity to classes, and social atmosphere.

# Off-Campus Housing

## The Lowdown On...
## Off-Campus Housing

**Undergrads Living Off Campus**
64%

**Freshmen Living Off Campus**
6%

**Average Off-Campus Room & Board**
$10,241

**Average Rents**
Studio: $1,100
1 BR: $1,280
2 BR: $1,700

**Best Time to Look for a Place**
Try to secure a place before spring break—early February is a good time to start the process.

## Popular Areas

Brentwood
Santa Monica
Westwood, especially on
Midvale, Gayley, Kelton, or
Landfair

## Students Speak Out On...
# Off-Campus Housing

### Q Westwood - a Village for University Students

The village surrounding the UCLA campus, Westwood Village, comprises blocks and blocks of high-rise apartment buildings and shared homes. There is really something for everyone. The options for off-campus housing are immense, whether you're looking for an apartment for many people or a room to share, many different set-ups are available. The cost of living is high but appropriate/reasonable for being in such a convenient and safe area (near Bel-Air/Beverly Hills and walking distance to three grocery stores, many restaurants, two movie theaters, several banks, FedEx/post office, shops, and countless bus stops). Many students live in the same general vicinity, which creates a sense of camaraderie, and the area is only about a 15-20 minute walk to campus. A car is not necessary to get around, but parking on the streets is common, and almost all of the buildings have parking (for a price).

### Q Off-Campus Housing Is Great!

They're all owned by UCLA, at least the ones close to campus. They're cheap and clean.

### Q Apartments Vary in Prices Depending on Location

There are different price ranges, depending on which side you're on and which you prefer. North of Wilshire on the dorm side are the party apartments and they are expensive, crowded, and have no parking. North of Wilshire on the campus side is very quiet. It is usually the same price but is really close to campus. It has no parking, as well. South of Wilshire, the apartments have some parking and are relatively big in size, but they are far from campus. Shuttles are available only at certain times.

## Q Family Housing

Overall, the affordability, proximity to campus, amenities, and quality of the family housing are outstanding and make a difference to my overall ability to be successful.

## Q Apartments Are Available!

It doesn't seem to be hard to get an apartment close to campus if you want one!

## Q Housing

There is variety and an abundance of housing near the school.

## Q Easy Apartments

The big plus about off-campus housing is that parking spots are usually included! The off-campus apartments are near classes and campus. I have the convenience of a dorm but get to do my own thing!

## Q Close to Campus

It's easy to find room in the University's off-campus housing system, and the apartments are closer to campus than some dorms!

### The College Prowler Take On...
# Off-Campus Housing

Off-campus housing prices are high in Westwood, but for many students, the proximity to classes and activities is worth it—in many cases, the apartments are closer to the dining halls and classrooms than the dorms! Apartments are also incredibly close to the party scene, and many three-room places morph into parties themselves. Parking is usually included, which is a giant plus when considering the miserable parking scenario on campus. To combat steep rent and the competitive vibe of popular buildings, students typically share Westwood rooms that could be found for lower prices in Brentwood or Santa Monica.

Moving to a place slightly farther away from campus has its pros and cons. Although many warn of the "commute" when living farther from campus, time isn't an issue with a car or public transportation. If you know the bus schedule and live near a stop, you can get to school in the same amount of time as people who walk from Westwood. Places like West Los Angeles are out of the UCLA bubble zone, so they boast a quieter and more mature, independent atmosphere. However, for students who crave involvement with their Bruin cronies, the social cost of living far from campus is too high.

**B**

**The College Prowler® Grade on**

**Off-Campus Housing: B**

A high grade in Off-Campus Housing indicates that apartments are of high quality, close to campus, affordable, and easy to secure.

www.collegeprowler.com

# Diversity

The Lowdown On...
## Diversity

**African American**
4%

**Native American**
0%

**Asian American**
38%

**White**
34%

**Hispanic**
15%

**Unknown**
5%

**International**
5%

**Out-of-State Students**
10%

## Faculty Diversity

African American: 2%
Asian American: 22%
Hispanic: 5%
International: 1%
Native American: 0%
White: 67%
Unknown: 2%

## Historically Black College/University?

No

## Student Age Breakdown

Under 18: 1%
18-19: 25%
20-21: 30%
22-24: 17%
25+: 27%

## Economic Status

Unlike some top-notch universities, the economic status of Bruins is varied. Nobody's ashamed to disclose their reliance on financial aid, and few flaunt their wealth. People seem to place more emphasis on character than money.

## Gay Pride

There is a LGBT Resource Center on campus, and there is a Lesbian, Gay, Bisexual, and Transgender Studies Program. However, with such a varied campus, it's a wonder students aren't more accepting of the many gay pride demonstrations that occur. Nobody's outright hateful of homosexuals, but nobody openly embraces them, either.

## Most Common Religions

UCLA's religious displays are overwhelmingly Christian, though Jewish and Muslim students occupy a large social space, as well. Bible studies are plentiful for those interested, and Hillel (the Jewish student center) bakes and sells very popular Challah bread each Friday.

## Political Activity

Whenever policies are instated that affect campus, you can bet a club will host an all-out protest. Rallies, megaphone-yellings, and marches are commonplace as students blast their respective political ideologies. Though they can get obnoxious, it's nice to be reminded of the aware and active attitude of the student body.

## Minority Clubs on Campus

The minority clubs at UCLA are a political juggernaut on campus—minority students have pride and aren't afraid to encourage change with rallies and protests. There is a political action group at UCLA that mainly comprises the minority clubs and associations on campus.

## Students Speak Out On...
# Diversity

### Q Swimming in Diversity

Every day, without exception, I hear a conversation in another language or experience a cultural shock as I make my way to class. UCLA is brimming with people all over the world with unique styles of life, and I love it! For someone whose school was predominantly Latino, this environment is not only opening my eyes to whole new ideas, but is teaching me to acknowledge that faraway worlds are more connected than they might first appear.

### Q It's Diverse!

I know people of so many races.

### Q Club Hopping

UCLA has a really diverse community. It seems like all races and religions are represented, and there's a club for everyone. Ethnicities are big on broadcasting themselves here via clubs or events.

### Q Not all Rich

UCLA is known for its diversity, and there is definitely a lot of it. I was surprised by the huge range of economic statuses represented here. There's also a ton of exchange students, and the nationality mix is awesome.

### Q Accepting and Tolerant

I'd say there are more ethnic backgrounds represented at UCLA than any school I've visited. People are very accepting, too.

## Q  Its a Small Country Itself.

When I arrived in LA, I never thought I could meet so many people. There are people from nearly every country in the world. It's so nice to find different people with different background making groups, partying, and studying together. I feel like UCLA is its own small world.

## Q  UCLA Is Very Diverse

Nearly every race, religion, and political belief is represented on campus. Although some may complain of a population dominated by Asian students or the under-representation of blacks, everyone finds their place at UCLA.

## Q  Mindblowing

The community here is incredibly diverse. Not only in terms of its international student body, but UCLA managed to put together an atmosphere that provides a comfortable environment for any person, any idea, and any view, allowing everyone to mix and empower the students to have a wider perspective of the world.

# The College Prowler Take On...
## Diversity

UCLA's campus is one of the most diverse in the United States. There are several resource centers on campus for minority students and anyone who wants to learn about other cultures, including the Center for African American Studies, American Indian Students Center, Asian American Studies Center, and the LGBT Campus Resource Center, and there are interesting cultural exhibitions and shows available weekly. There are also plenty of minority student clubs on campus, including the Afrikan Student Union, Asian Pacific Coalition, and MEChA (for Hispanic students).

But, while UCLA is home to students from varied backgrounds, it seems like most tend to mingle within their own ethnic groups. When it does occur, racial bonding is facilitated by intramural sports, parties, and interest-based clubs. Some people are intimidated by ethnic clubs and are hesitant to embrace other cultures, and the vocalization of minority groups can make them seem more plentiful than they really are. But, making a friend for life with a person of another race is definitely possible if you're willing to cross the occasionally rough barrier.

**B+**

**The College Prowler® Grade on**

Diversity: B+

A high grade in Diversity indicates that ethnic minorities and international students have a notable presence on campus and that students of different economic backgrounds, religious beliefs, and sexual preferences are well-represented.

# Guys & Girls

### The Lowdown On...
## Guys & Girls

**Female Undergrads**
55%

**Male Undergrads**
45%

## Birth Control Available?

Yes: Birth control pills are available at Arthur Ashe Student Health and Wellness Center.


## Social Scene

Although UCLA prides itself on its diversity and social students, it should be noted that students are really only outgoing within their respective groupings—social circle, major, or Greek house. However, courtesy and general friendliness are traits of almost all Bruins.


## Hookups or Relationships?

At a school this big, it's not hard to find someone with the same romantic goals as yours, and you can find both the carousing hook-up seekers and serious mate-finders here. Plenty of students merely hook up on weekends, while others settle down into quite serious relationships, usually with fellow Bruins and occasionally with significant others from neighboring schools.


## Dress Code

The sizzling California sunshine and mild winters call for casual clothes to class. T-shirts, flip-flops, jeans, and workout gear are the norm—anything more might get stares. However, even though the red carpet is a few miles down Sunset, UCLA students sometimes dress like stars to go out. Guys don jeans and nice shirts, while girls rock heels, designer tops, and mini (we're talking mini) skirts. However, this is SoCal and casualness is always accepted—nobody's snubbed for their attire.

## Did You Know?

Best Places to Meet Guys & Girls:

- Maloney's
- Frat parties
- Class (it's UCLA—everyone goes!)
- Club sports

Best Places to Hook Up:

- Frats
- Private study rooms in dorms/libraries
- Powell Library basement
- Sculpture Garden
- Apartment parties

## Students Speak Out On...
# Guys & Girls

### Q Diverse
The relationships are so diverse here. Everyone is different and everyone dresses different, yet we all interact, accept, and love our differences.

### Q UCLA Girls
UCLA girls are very attractive. Guys, I would say, are attractive, too. Overall, it's a great school to meet people, and the weather allows for everyone to show off a little skin.

### Q Fun People
Most guys who are in a frat or play a sport are always down to go out and have fun. There are way more blonde girls here than at home! Everyone gets along really well and has friends in a bunch of different groups.

### Q Academically Competive, Beachy Cool, Trendy Nights
Student life at UCLA exemplifies what one would expect of student life in sunny southern California. Many students thrive in the intensely competitive academic environment, which is offset by the beachy cool of California and the trendiness of Los Angeles.

### Q Friendly Environment Wherever I Go
Throughout my experience, I have always met friendly faces. Perhaps it may be because I tend to approach people in a friendly manner, but the people I encounter are friendly and helpful. They dress in comfy clothes, as they know there is no need to impress others in an academic environment. Everyone is able to join groups that interest

them and hang out with those with similar tastes in things. The relationships between one another can ultimately end up close. It's like one big, happy family.

## Q Looks Pricey

The guys and girls vary in appearance. However, in general, there tends to be more Asian and white students, with very few African American students. Almost everyone dresses in quality clothes. I can tell that both the guys and girls shop in expensive stores. Specifics depend on what part of campus you're on. For example, on North campus (art, photography, cinema, theater), there are some pretty creative dressers with lots of color and layers of pants and skirts and scarves. The guys tend to wear tight pants.

## Q Guys Can be Cocky, Girls are Great

Guys here are kind of on a power trip. They are not used to girls flocking them, which can sometimes lead to cockiness. Girls are really cute, fit, and put together. Oh wait, and super smart!

## Q Diverse Set of Friends

There are people who stay in their rooms and study 24/7, and there are the very social kids who go out practically every night. The boys are cute—they're from California!

The College Prowler Take On...
# Guys & Girls

Despite rumors of superficialness and the proximity of Hollywood, guys and girls at UCLA are a down-to-earth and diverse bunch. There really is no average Bruin—students encompass a range of backgrounds, and most want to learn about each others'. Though separation between larger social cliques like the Greek system or minority groups is common, spontaneous chit-chat and phone number exchanges between guys and girls occur often. There are more attractive girls than guys at UCLA, but nobody can really complain due to the sheer number of romantic interests at a school with 25,000 undergrads.

Being in Southern California certainly boosts UCLA's grades for hotness. Students take care of themselves and are always tan and groomed. The gym is the place to see and be seen—Bruins of both sexes don't mess around when it comes to treadmills. When guy-to-girl interaction goes beyond the ever-prominent party hookup, it's usually in the form of an LA café date or Westwood movie outing. Many students are eager to enter relationships, and many do.

Guys: A-

**The College Prowler®
Grade on
Guys & Girls**

A high grade for Guys or Girls indicates that the students on campus is attractive, smart, friendly, and engaging, and that the school has a decent gender ratio.

Girls: A-

# Athletics

**The Lowdown On...**
## Athletics

### Athletic Association
NAA
NCAA

### Athletic Division
NCAA Division I-A

### Athletic Conferences
Football: Pacific-10
Conference
Basketball: Pacific-10
Conference

### School Colors
Blue and gold

### School Nickname/ Mascot
Bruin

### Men Playing Varsity Sports
437: 4%

## Women Playing Varsity Sports

415: 3%

## Men's Varsity Sports

Baseball
Basketball
Football
Golf
Soccer
Tennis
Track and field
Volleyball
Water polo

## Women's Varsity Sports

Basketball
Golf
Gymnastics
Rowing
Soccer
Softball
Swimming and diving
Tennis
Track and field
Volleyball
Water polo

## Intramurals

Basketball
Dodgeball
Flag football
Soccer
Softball
Ultimate Frisbee
Volleyball

## Club Sports

Archery
Badminton
Baseball
Bowling
Cycling
Dragon boat
Equestrian
Fencing
Ice hockey
Kendo
Lacrosse
Powerlifting
Rowing
Rugby
Running
Sailing
Skiing and snowboarding
Soccer
Softball
Surfing
Swimming
Table tennis
Taekwondo
Tennis
Triathlon
Ultimate Frisbee
Volleyball
Water polo
Waterskiing and wakeboarding
Wrestling
Wushu

## Students Receiving Athletic Financial Aid

Football: 87
Basketball: 29

Baseball: 30
Cross Country/Track: 69
Other Sports: 167

## Graduation Rates of Athletic Financial Aid Recipients

Football: 50%
Basketball: 67%
Baseball: 60%
Cross Country/Track: 75%
Other Sports: 68%

## Athletic Fields & Facilities

Acosta Athletic Training Center
Drake Stadium
Easton Stadium
Jackie Robinson Stadium
JD Morgan Center
John Wooden Center
Los Angeles Tennis Center
Pauley Pavilion
Rose Bowl
Spieker Aquatics Center
Sunset Canyon Recreation Center
UCLA Boathouse

## Most Popular Sports

UCLA truly is a two-sport school. During the fall quarter, students crowd Rose Bowl-bound buses for well-attended football games, though most of the fun is had at tailgate parties. In the winter, basketball dominates the sports scene, with Bruins commonly camping out for courtside seating.

## Most Overlooked Teams

The softball team is constantly winning championships without many students taking notice. The same goes for men's track and field and men's and women's water polo—these teams are always competitive and rarely receive publicity. Rugby and gymnastics are rising in popularity among student spectators.

## School Spirit

Students are proud to be accepted into UCLA, and their zest for the University's academic side seems to evolve into unadulterated school spirit during sports seasons. The dorms light up as the sports teams charge into the national spotlight, lines for buses to the Rose Bowl are miles long, and blue and gold apparel is literally everywhere. Although the basketball and football teams don't always win championships, students still gush about the lore UCLA carries. Most students engage in sporting events either by actually going to the games or watching with friends at Maloney's. If the big game against USC ever comes up, be ready for some real student spirit to spill. The Beat 'SC Bonfire is an event with several thousand students that even captivates the local media.

## Getting Tickets

A lottery ticket package system previously reigned, but the 2010-11 sports season will usher in the $99 Den Sports Pass. If purchased, the pass will grant students access to all UCLA sporting events—if they arrive early enough to beat their fellow Bruin fans in the seating war. And, while students were previously able to purchase sports tickets at a discounted rate, the new system will leave pass-less Bruins with no choice but to buy tickets at the public, albeit fairly reasonable, price.

## Best Place to Take a Walk

North Campus's sculpture garden is serene, yet small. The seven-acre Botanical Gardens are always peaceful, and active students love to walk or jog "The Perimeter," an unofficial 3.8-mile course around campus.

## Did You Know?

UCLA has won more NCAA championships than any other university in the country.

## Students Speak Out On...
# Athletics

### Q Best Athletics!
We have the best teams!

### Q Amazing School Spirit
UCLA's top competitor is USC and that keeps the school spirit very high. At football, basketball, and volleyball games against USC, UCLA students rally to show support for their teams. Overall, the campus is very athletic, and there are many programs and athletic facilities available to all students.

### Q School Spirit
UCLA students have a lot of school spirit!

### Q There Is No Shortage of Sports Events
Sporting events, except for football and men's basketball, are completely free for students, and there is an incredible amount of school spirit for all sports.

### Q Amazing School Spirit
the games are always great because of the fans. we have a huge local fan base and an intense rivalry which makes it all the more fun. the student section is always incredibly lively and is what makes the games so fun.

### Q Hugely Spirited Pac 10 School
Though UCLA teams are not always the best, there aren't many universities that rival our school spirit. The athletic facilities are top-notch, and the fan support is unbeatable.

## School Athletics

Here at UCLA, most of the students dwell in athletics. This is probably due to the NCAA; this school has participated in many competitions and won. Therefore, students are motivated. Several of them are involved in sports such as Basketball, Volleyball, Football, Tennis, Gymnastics, Martial Arts, etc. Students participate in sports programs for personal reasons, or for the sake of being on a team.

## Best Basketball Varsity Team Ever!!

Many people are crazy about wathcing basketball games.

# The College Prowler Take On...
# Athletics

Varsity sports are what initially put UCLA on the map, and the fact that the school boasts more than 100 NCAA championships instills an insane amount of spirit in all Bruins right off the bat. Basketball usually lives up to the hype, as the team has the storied lore of Wooden to attain each year. Yet in the fall, the Rose Bowl is full of diehards in complete denial of UCLA's often meager football performance. Students attend the games to indulge in the frenzied action, and the ticket availability fluctuates with the success of the team. And while barrages of spirited students don't typically attend them, it surely shouldn't be forgotten that top-notch sporting events from rugby to gymnastics are hosted almost daily on campus.

Whether it is UCLA's varsity success, outdoor formatting, or sunny SoCal weather, exercise is a student priority, and the up-to-date Wooden Center is often more crowded than a frat party. IM sports have different tiers of competition, usually separated into three levels, but almost nobody competes in them besides Greek teams attempting to prove who's the coolest. The club sports scene, however, is well-respected and very competitive.

**The College Prowler® Grade on**

Athletics: B+

A high grade in Athletics indicates that students have school spirit, that sports programs are respected, that games are well-attended, and that intramurals are a prominent part of student life.

# Nightlife

The Lowdown On...
## Nightlife

**Cheapest Place to Get a Drink**
O'Hara's

**Primary Areas with Nightlife**
Melrose
Santa Monica
Sunset Strip
West Hollywood

**Closing Time**
2 a.m.

**Useful Resources for Nightlife**
www.groovetickets.com
www.la.com/nightlife
www.lanightlife.com

# Club Listings

## Circus Disco

6655 Santa Monica Blvd.
Hollywood
(323) 462-1291
*www.circusdisco.com*
This place is a gold mine of musical talent, especially on Saturday nights with Spundae. The world-class DJs keep the place on its feet, and it has been nominated for best dance club in Los Angeles. There are multiple rooms, so the music changes from location to location. The thundering bass and electronic vibes will surely keep your legs pumping and swaying all the way home.

## Club DV8

Hollywood and Highland, level 3
Downtown LA
(323) 461-2017
*www.kiisfm.com/pages/dv8.html*
Run by KIIS FM, LA's Top 40 radio station, DV8 is a popular Thursday and Friday destination because it's 18-and-up.

## The Ivar

6356 Hollywood Blvd.
Hollywood
(323) 465-4827
*ivarhollywood.com*
The Ivar is in the heart of Hollywood and is one block west of the world's most famous intersection, Hollywood and Vine. The architecture is spellbinding, and the club is enormous, with enough space to fit 1,500 people. Clubgoers beware: There is usually a stiflingly long line outside if you arrive past 10:30 p.m.

## Les Deux

1638 N. Las Palmas Ave.
Downtown LA
(323) 462-7674
*dolcegroup.com*
Seen on various not-to-be-named LA reality shows, Les Deux is an ultra-trendy club perfect for a big night out or birthday. Top 40 hits will be blaring Thursday, Friday, and Saturday nights.

## Spaceland

1717 Silverlake Blvd.
Silver Lake
(310) 661-4380
*www.clubspaceland.com*
Spaceland is the destination for techno and house beats, as well as up-and-coming local bands, which debut here almost nightly.

## The Viper Room

8852 W. Sunset Blvd.
Downtown LA
(310) 358-1881

*viperroom.com*
The Viper Room has a more upscale vibe than the typical student dive, but the club's killer drinks and often killer alternative bands are worth the extra buck.

## Whiskey A Go Go
8901 W. Sunset Blvd.
Downtown LA
(310) 652-4202
*www.whiskyagogo.com*
This cozy venue is a jumping-off point for dozens of local bands, and a ticket and drink won't cost upwards of $20. Although it's on Sunset, Whiskey's vibe is anything but obnoxiously trendy.

# Bar Listings
## The Colony
1743 Cahuenga Blvd.
Hollywood
(323) 525-2450
*www.sbe.com/thecolony*
The Colony is in the space formerly occupied by White Lotus. The Colony is billed as "The Hamptons meets Hollywood," and the decor follows this theme. There are wood-plank floors, an outdoor garden, and a large dance floor.

## O'Hara's
1000 Gayley Ave.
Westwood
(310) 208-1942
Formerly called Maloney's, this bar houses the most TVs in all of Westwood and is an absolute madhouse whenever there is a sporting event. Student sports fans (and older ones who can't let go of their college roots) will find O'Hara's the place to be for any sporting occasion.

## Tengu
10853 Lindbrook Dr.
Westwood
(310) 209-0071
*www.tengu.com*
Named after a group of elusive long-nosed goblins in Japanese folklore, Tengu is a very hot Asian-fusion restaurant, as well as a great bar. Sundays are half-price sake nights and there is no cover charge.

## W Bar
930 Hilgard Ave. in W Hotel
(310) 208-8765
This bar offers a modern, chic alternative to the loud and student-saturated local bar scene. Set in the amazing W Hotel, a first-class building of its own, the ambiance of the bar is more New York than UCLA. The velvet ropes may be intimidating, but the

intimacy inside is stunning, especially on the weekdays. For a date that's slightly out of the ordinary, check out this swanky yet subtle jewel tucked away on the outskirts of Westwood.

### Westwood Brewing Company

1097 Glendon Ave.
Westwood
(310) 209-2739
Skip the bottlenecks in favor of one of their handcrafted ales like a Westwood Blonde or Pear Cider. This is the only microbrewery in Westwood, so enjoy the variety here. Happy hour is from 3 p.m. to 7 p.m. with $2.50 beers and half-priced appetizers. On Sundays from 11 a.m. to 3 p.m., come here to watch some football with $2 pints and Bloody Marys, 25-cent Buffalo wings. There's live entertainment every night and no cover charge.

## Other Places to Check Out

Hollywood Canteen
Saddle Ranch
The Sunset Room

## Local Specialties

Microbrews from Westwood Brewing Company

## Favorite Drinking Games

Beer Pong
Card games
Century Club
Flip Cup
Power Hour
Quarters

## What to Do if You're Not 21

### The Cow's End Café

34 Washington Blvd.
Marina Del Rey
(310) 574-1080
*www.thecowsendcafe.com*
There are plenty of comfy couches and delicious smoothies here to melt away daily stress while you curl up with a good book. The local crowd is relaxed, and on certain nights there are live performances. The Cow's End also houses a computer with Internet connection for some quick e-mail check-ups, and plug-ins. Beware of the loud writers talking to studio heads about their prospective manuscripts—while amusing, these people are extraordinarily loud in the otherwise tranquil atmosphere.

### Crash Mansion

1024 S. Grand Ave.
Downtown
(213) 747-0999
*www.crashmansionla.com*
This is one of downtown LA's premiere club venues. The balcony is a cool place to chill and get your drink on with

another full bar in the middle. The club is modern and definitely large in scale. There are plenty of students from all over Los Angeles at this club.

## Organization Parties

The UCLA Party Network is a campus organization run by some savvy students who arrange for entrance into LA's nightclubs for groups of Bruins who pay a modest fee. Hummer limos are the usual method of transport for these Thursday night excursions.

## Students Speak Out On...
# Nightlife

### Q Parties
Frat parties, club parties, and house parties are a lot of fun!

### Q It's Los Angeles- You Can Find SOMETHING
Between the clubs on Sunset and the concert venues located all over town, it's easy to find something to do. There are also movie premieres and screenings in Hollywood, and comedy clubs and late-night diners to hang out in. You just have to pick up a paper and look at the events section. There's bound to be something you'll enjoy.

### Q Amazing
It's so amazing, I can't remember much. Just kidding.

### Q No Boredom!
There's truly something for everyone here. Younger students hang out at frats or party in dorms, and upperclassmen go to the zillions of bars in LA. It's the perfect social setup. Once you get tired of a certain scene, there's always a new venue to try out. I can't imagine getting bored.

### Q Party All You Want
If you want to party, you can always find a party. There are clubs almost everywhere and you dont need to be 21, just 18 is good enough. And there are always people throwing parties, so no need to worry about nightlife.

## Q Awesome!

Westwood is amazing with lots of different things to do—movies, food, and buses going everywhere else you would want to go.

## Q Frat Parties

There are a multitude of fraternities and clubs on campus, so there are tons of parties during the week. They are always filled with lots students and are a perfect way to spend an evening.

## Q Diverse Nightlife

There is no shortage of apartment and fraternity parties in Westwood. Thursday nights are big going-out nights, especially for Greek parties. The Westwood bar scene is limited with two bars, but that also makes it fun. Bars can be crowded but you're guaranteed to know the people there and pretty much always guaranteed a good time.

## The College Prowler Take On...
# Nightlife

There seems to be a party for everyone on and around campus. Between frats, athlete houses, apartments, and dorms, weekends offer a plethora of red-cup opportunities. For underclassmen, the allure of frats and wild apartment parties are major draws, although only girls can truly float freely between gatherings. Guys may have a tougher time being allowed into parties with which they're not affiliated, so Westwood bars become a popular resort. The Village's two breweries are cozy and cheap getaways for upperclassmen, and it's a guarantee that you'll find a solid half of your Facebook friends milling about by the bar.

As far as off-campus entertainment, downtown clubs are only a costly cab ride or sober driver away. Most are pricey with long lines, but deep-pocketed upperclassmen often venture to the Sunset Strip with success. If trendy clubs aren't your thing, there are plenty of diversions, galleries, jumbo cinemas, and outdoor malls to hold your interest by night.

A-

**The College Prowler® Grade on**

Nightlife: A-

A high grade in Nightlife indicates that there are many bars and clubs in the area that are easily accessible and affordable. Other determining factors include the number of options for the under-21 crowd and the prevalence of house parties.

# Greek Life

### The Lowdown On...
## Greek Life

**Freshman Men in Fraternities**
11%

**Freshman Women in Sororities**
11%

**Undergrad Men in Fraternities**
13%

**Undergrad Women in Sororities**
13%

**Number of Fraternities**
33

**Number of Sororities**
31

## Fraternities

Alpha Epsilon Omega
Alpha Epsilon Pi
Alpha Gamma Omega
Alpha Phi Alpha
Beta Theta Pi
Delta Kappa Epsilon
Delta Lambda Phi
Delta Phi Beta
Delta Sigma Phi
Delta Tau Delta
Gamma Zeta Alpha
Kappa Alpha Psi
Lambda Chi Alpha
Lambda Phi Epsilon
Nu Alpha Kappa
Omega Sigma Tau
Phi Delta Theta
Phi Kappa Psi
Pi Kappa Alpha
Pi Kappa Phi
Sigma Alpha Epsilon
Sigma Chi
Sigma Lambda Beta
Sigma Nu
Sigma Phi Epsilon
Sigma Pi
Sigma Pi Sigma
Theta Chi
Theta Delta Chi
Theta Xi
Triangle
Zeta Beta Tau
Zeta Phi Rho

## Sororities

Alpha Chi Omega
Alpha Delta Chi
Alpha Delta Pi
Alpha Epsilon Phi
Alpha Gamma Alpha
Alpha Phi
Chi Alpha Delta
Chi Delta Theta
Chi Omega
Delta Delta Delta
Delta Gamma
Delta Phi Beta
Delta Sigma Theta
Gamma Phi Beta
Gamma Rho Lambda
Kappa Alpha Theta
Kappa Delta
Kappa Kappa Gamma
Kappa Psi Epsilon
Lambda Theta Alpha
Lambda Theta Nu
Phi Lambda Rho
Pi Beta Phi
Sigma Alpha Epsilon Pi
Sigma Alpha Zeta
Sigma Delta Sigma
Sigma Gamma Rho
Sigma Lambda Gamma
Sigma Pi Sigma
Tau Theta Pi
Theta Kappa Phi

## Multicultural Colonies

Alpha Epsilon Omega
Alpha Gamma Alpha
Chi Alpha Delta
Chi Delta Theta
Delta Phi Beta
Gamma Zeta Alpha
Kappa Psi Epsilon
Lambda Phi Epsilon
Lambda Theta Alpha
Lambda Theta Nu
Nu Alpha Kappa

Omega Sigma Tau
Phi Lambda Rho
Sigma Alpha Epsilon Pi
Sigma Alpha Zeta
Sigma Delta Sigma
Sigma Lambda Beta
Sigma Lambda Gamma
Sigma Pi Beta
Sigma Pi Sigma
Tau Theta Pi
Theta Kappa Phi
Zeta Phi Rho

## Other Greek Organizations

Asian Greek Council
GAMMA
Interfraternity Council
Latino Greek Council
Multi-Interest Greek Council
National Pan-Hellenic Council
Order of Omega
Panhellenic Council

## Did You Know?

The ABC TV series "Greek" is often filmed on campus, and the show's story line is rumored to revolve around real events in the UCLA Greek system.

## Students Speak Out On...
# Greek Life

### Q  Go Frats!
Greeks at UCLA are not as bad as everyone thinks they are. You are usually welcome at any frat party if you're a girl, and guys are nice, too.

### Q  Best Part of My UCLA Life
As a member of Greek life, I love being in a house. I have met tons of people, had a great social life, and have formed lasting friendships with the girls in my house. That being said, many students who are not members of Greek life look poorly on the organization as a whole. The UCLA community is hostile to the Greeks, and many people do not understand that we do much more than party.

### Q  Greek Life at UCLA
Greek life is a great way to make a lot of amazing friends and make UCLA a more manageable community. There are plenty of parties if that's what you're interested in, and there are also plenty of other ways to be involved in philanthropies around campus. UCLA Greek life is not like Greek life at a state school. UCLA students put an emphasis on school, and sorority life is a later priority. We are all dedicated to our studies as much as our houses.

### Q  Non-Greek
Greek life is very prominent, and it makes things exciting and interesting. However, it's not for me.

### Q  Greeeeeeeeeeeeks
The Greek life is relatively strong here. About 13 percent of the people are involved in Greek life, but since there are so many students, chances are that you will know someone

from a house. Fraternities and sororities are located on different streets, on Gayley and Hilgard, respectively. I don't find that Greeks and non-Greeks are loved or hated by one another—everyone is fine with each other!

## Q Not the Stereotypical Scene
People perceive rushing a sorority or frat as a judgemental experience, but honestly, lots of houses here are very down-to-earth and the members are nice people.

## Q Greek or Bust
Most of the most fun parties are centered on frats, so if you're a girl, it's helpful to be in a sorority.

## Q There's a House for Everyone
Greek life tends to run the social scene, so if you're in a house, it's going to be a good time. There's definitely a frat or sorority for everyone—they're really diverse.

# The College Prowler Take On...
# Greek Life

Greek Bruins try to make it a point to show that they're not the letter-wearing, keg-chugging animals stereotyped on TV. And to some extent, this is true—when chatting up a sorority girl or frat guy, you know there's a UCLA-worthy brain in there. There's little hierarchy or cliquey-ness to be found within Bruin frats and sororities, though the Greek system itself often acts as a giant, everyone-knows-and-loves-each-other family to which other students are merely foreigners. Most agree that the process of joining one of UCLA's many nationally recognized houses can be daunting, but the years of camaraderie, networking opportunities, and feel-good service ventures are worth it.

As far as Greeks and the social scene goes, frat parties tend to make up a large part of weekend activity and are often the only alternative to low-key apartment gatherings. If you're a member of Greek life, this means you're constantly ambushed with raging opportunities, while non-Greeks may just have to watch from the sidelines. Greeks typically also attend two official events per week, such as date parties, philanthropy events, or club-centered "raids" with other houses. However, students who choose not to partake in Greek parties still find themselves with all of L.A. to conquer by night—the Sunset Strip and Santa Monica are popular party destinations and only a car or bus ride away.

**A+**

**The College Prowler® Grade on**

Greek Life: A+

A high grade in Greek Life indicates that sororities and fraternities are not only present, but also active on campus. Other determining factors include the variety of houses available and the respect the Greek community receives from the rest of the campus.

# Drug Scene

The Lowdown On...
## Drug Scene

**Most Popular Drugs**
Adderall
Alcohol
Cocaine
Ecstasy
Marijuana

**Alcohol-Related
Referrals**
379

**Alcohol-Related
Arrests**
3

**Drug-Related Referrals**
103

**Drug-Related Arrests**
18

# Drug Counseling Programs
## Counseling and Psychological Services (CAPS)
John Wooden Center West, 221 Westwood Plaza
(310) 825-0768
Group counseling, individual counseling

## Student Psychological Services
John Wooden Center West
(310) 825-7291
Screening tests, brief interventions

### Students Speak Out On...
# Drug Scene

### Q Drinking

There is a lot of drinking going on in and around the frats, but otherwise, on campus, people are very safe and sober. Smoking is not as common and usually done in private.

### Q Drugs and Alcohol Not So Visible

The drug and alcohol scene doesn't really exist at UCLA, unless you go looking for it. Sure, there are parties that have drugs and alcohol, but most of them are off campus and if you want to stay completely away from them, it is very easy.

### Q Lots of It.

I live off campus, just a block from it. There are so many parties! People drink like there's no tomorrow. The partying happens mostly Thursday through Sunday. That's when it's the loudest. Many people who drink at these parties also smoke herb. It is very common to do those two things. There is a number of people, however, who don't party or who just drink water or juice and might smoke little to none. Some people were into drugs before coming to this school and they bring that attitude with them. Once a friend of mine come to campus tripping on LSD. This is rare, however. Doing drugs seems to be most common with north campus students.

### Q Eh . . . nothing is out in open

You can get drugs if you're interested, but nothing's really out in the open. Weed is usually at frat parties, but that's the only drug that's visible.

## ℚ Just Drinking

People drink and some smoke pot. I have never seen people doing any sort of hard drug or ever been asked to try them, and I consider myself a very social person. Any drugs that do go on are hush-hush because users know the students don't think it's acceptable. Mostly people just have an awesome time and get drunk.

## ℚ Smoking Is Most Prevalent

Although not throughout campus, it is prevalent outside Powel.

## ℚ Drug Use Is Not Very Visible

The drug scene at UCLA is very small and is barely visible at all to the general student population. I have not come in contact with any hard drugs at all, although they do exist. Drinking is far more prevalent.

## ℚ Average

UCLA isn't a dry campus, but if you're acting stupidly drunk or high in public, the UCPD will definitely arrest you. If you look/act fine, then you'll be fine. Peer pressure isn't too bad; people do what they want.  It's clear that it exists on campus, and it's funny to watch the drunk people come back to campus on Thursday nights and get food at BruCaf. Pot and cocaine seem to be the most popular drugs at UCLA.

# The College Prowler Take On...
# Drug Scene

Either a drug scene doesn't exist at UCLA or students are just so super-smart that they can hide it extremely well. Though they're available if you know where to look, hard drugs simply aren't out in the open. The only exception is finals week, when, in true UCLA fashion, dozens of dedicated Bruins pop Adderall in a quest to conquer that fifth all-nighter in a row. Though other drugs are hard to come by, people certainly don't hesitate to blaze next to, around, and (gasp!) on campus, but care is taken to avoid the constantly perusing UC Police. UCLA is by no means a stoner school, but students seem to over-indulge on weed to make up for the lack of visible hard drugs. And, of course, there is the ever-visible alcohol, which no Bruin will ever have a hard time tracking down.

Off-campus drug usage is common for students who want to explore the medium. Marijuana is the most available drug, followed by ecstasy, then cocaine. Most students do not plunge further into the realm of drug usage beyond that, and classes require more attention than the daily use of drugs allows.

**The College Prowler® Grade on**

Drug Scene: C-

A high grade in the Drug Scene indicates that drugs are not a noticeable part of campus life; drug use is not visible, and no pressure to use them seems to exist.

# Campus Strictness

The Lowdown On...
## Campus Strictness

### Students Are Most Likely to Get Caught...
Downloading copyrighted materials
Drinking or smoking in the dorms
Drinking underage
Having candles and incense sticks in your dorm
Making too much noise in your dorm
Not showing your ID when you enter the dorm
Parking illegally
Running stop signs
Skateboarding
Stealing food from the dorms

### Visitation Policies
In most dorms, visitors must be checked in at the front desk and need to be with their host when entering buildings. In

suite-style dorms, there really are no lobbies, so guests may enter as they please, making suites the ideal rooms for avid hosts. Visitation policies at UCLA are quite lenient, and they really do not impede visitors' fun.

### Students Speak Out On...
# Campus Strictness

### Q Not Strict
You can feel pretty much free to do anything you want that doesn't negatively affect the experience of others.

### Q Not Very Strict
They aren't very strict but they still make students feel safe.

### Q Crackdown
You will get caught if you are doing something against policy. Period. Most people are smart enough to figure this out after their first citation, but for second-time offenders, time spent in custody normally sobers them up pretty quick.

### Q Don't Sweat It
Drinking in the dorms is not allowed, but usually RAs don't mind as long as you're not being ridiculously loud/obnoxious. Everyone walks around between parties, and a few people I know have gotten MIPs, but usually the police are very student-friendly. Just don't walk around with open bottles.

### Q RAs Are Alright
RAs (resident assistants) aren't too strict in most of the dorms, but in others they can crack down often.

### Q Strict in Crowded Dorms
Though the campus is incredibly safe, RAs and building authorities are not that strict. In more crammed halls, people do get written up a lot for noise and drinking, but in more secluded dorms, nothing's really enforced.

## Q Lax but There if Necessary

The professors and building personnel are relatively lax, but they are definitely there if you need them. When you get in trouble in the dorms, not a lot of punishment is enacted, so it's not too troubling.

## Q Reasonable, Common-Sense Rules

You are allowed to drink in your room, as long as you don't make excessive noise or disturb other people. RAs tend to be extremely friendly and will only write you up for the most severe things.

# The College Prowler Take On...
# Campus Strictness

Though UCLA dubs itself a zero-tolerance institution, most Bruins find the authority system to be decently lax. While in Westwood and going between apartment parties, students should be cautious not to stumble or tote the ominous red cup because police (however lenient they may be) are always present. Cops have been known to break up such events as Undie Run, but the attitude toward them is generally one of tolerance, as they surely let students have their fun. And, of course, the UCPD responds quickly and efficiently when called. As far as parties, apartments get as rowdy as they like with hardly any police interference. The newly instated chancellor, however, has worked to institute policies that have severely decreased the intensity of Greek events and increased security at these parties.

Currently, security is relaxed in most dorms. Drinking in the rooms is arguably the No. 1 cause of citations, and punishment really depends on your respective RA's (resident assistant) attitude: some dish out hours of bathroom cleaning, and others inflict no sanctions at all. On most occasions, RAs are students too and respect their fellow Bruins' right to rage. If drinking is concealed and kept quiet in dorms, it's almost impossible to encounter trouble. Visitation policies make it easy to let guests share in the UCLA experience.

**The College Prowler® Grade on**

Campus
Strictness: B

A high Campus Strictness grade implies an overall lenient atmosphere; police and RAs are fairly tolerant, and the administration's rules are flexible.

# Parking

### The Lowdown On...
## Parking

### Parking Services
**Transporation and Parking**
555 Westwood Plaza
(310) 794-RIDE
*transportation@ts.ucla.edu*
*www.parking.ucla.edu*

### Approximate Parking Permit Cost
$99–$237 per quarter

### Student Parking Lot
Yes: Students can park in all campus parking lots except the medical center and otherwise marked spaces.

### Freshmen Allowed to Park
Yes: However, since permits are awarded based on factors, including class standing, it's very hard for freshmen to get permits.

## Common Parking Tickets

Expired meter: $50
Parking with invalid permit: $50
Fire lane: $65
No stopping zone: $65
Handicapped zone: $503

## Getting a Parking Permit

Students must apply for a parking pass by the fifth week of each quarter, and this deadline is as strictly enforced as UCLA's parking laws themselves. Parking is assigned on a points basis, with points coming from a student's class standing, living distance from school, employment status, willingness to carpool, and job's distance from campus. Permits are tough to get unless you have a legitimate job and have sophomore standing or above.

## Did You Know?

Best Places to Find a Parking Spot:

• In the evenings, you can park on Westholme Drive or Midvale Avenue, both of which are a quick walk from campus.

• In the morning and early afternoon, Lot 6 or metered parking near North Campus are your best bets, but a long shot at that.

• It's usually worth the headache to buy a pass in Lot 11 or Lot 36 and take a shuttle into campus.

## Students Speak Out On...
# Parking

### Q Difficult

Since UCLA is such a big school, it is hard to get around and find places to park. Freshmen and sophomores have it hardest because they cannot drive or use their cars if they live in an on-campus dorm.

### Q Parking Permits Required!

You need a permit to even park near the school. The best way to get one is to say that you have a job on weekends outside of Los Angeles, or say that you're commuting.

### Q Avoid Hassles With Cars

Invest in a bike instead! There isn't a dire need to have a car. While cars are usually more efficient than the public transit systems, the traffic and the cost of parking aren't worth it. Parking costs a lot, but it is available. It is not worth parking in a space that you aren't supposed to be parked in either because the parking fines are nasty!  Avoid the costs, save the environment, and ditch the car.

### Q Need a Good Reason for a Permit

They don't let you get a permit even if you are willing to pay for it. They only allow people with jobs off campus or commuters to get one.

### Q Parking at UCLA Is Not Easy

Parking at UCLA is very inconvenient. Day passes are expensive, monthly permits are not very affordable on a student budget, and parking buildings are usually very crowded. However, there is no need for a car if you live on campus or in Westwood as everything that is not accessible on foot can be reached through the network of buses in the LA area.

### Q Don't Need a Car but Parking Is Expensive
The great thing about UCLA is that you do not need a car on campus. Westwood is a five-minute walk from campus, and Santa Monica is only a 10-minute bus ride. There is plenty of parking on campus, but it is difficult to get a parking permit to park on campus all year-round. However, there are parking spots available to park your car in Westwood year-round. The only problem is that this option is pretty expensive.

### Q Permits Hard to Get
Parking permits are nearly impossible to obtain if you don't have a job. Street parking can be very hard to find, and parking patrol gives out tickets readily.

### Q So Expensive
Parking is terrible, mostly because of the cost. There is no lack of parking, but guest parking is horrendous. If one is slightly over the time limit, it's an immediate ticket.

### The College Prowler Take On...
# Parking

One thing UCLA is not world-renowned for is parking. Students must apply for passes early in each quarter, and they are awarded based on factors such as employment and commuter zip codes. High class standing and a job are needed to secure a parking spot, but spaces are harder to come by than clouds in the LA sky. Many students are experts at faking the forms by pretending to have jobs and reaping the rewards, but since forgery is not encouraged, hit-or-miss parking can be found on Westwood side streets.

If you commute to UCLA, you can apply for the Carpool Parking Permit, which gives priority parking at a cheaper rate. Anyone can buy a night parking pass, which is good every day after 4 p.m. and all weekend. Still, the fact that Bruins can't find reliable parking at their own school is horrible. Daily non-permit parking on campus is $7, and after 8 a.m., you have to park in the lot off campus. There are also campus parking meters, but they only allow parking up to two hours—and good luck finding one during daylight hours. UCLA also loses major points for starting the free parking time on campus at 9 p.m.—and, unfortunately, these free spaces are only effective for extracurricular activities. But, really, what did you expect from a school in the heart of Los Angeles?

**The College Prowler® Grade on**

**Parking: C-**

A high grade in the Parking section indicates that parking is both available and affordable, and that parking enforcement isn't overly severe.

# Transportation

**The Lowdown On...**
## Transportation

### Best Ways to Get Around Town
Big Blue Bus
Hitch a ride from a friend.
Rollerblade from point A to point B.
Take a cab.

### Campus Shuttle
**Campus Express**
This shuttle runs counter-clockwise around campus, with stops at Weyburn Terrace and Macgowan Hall. A shuttle is scheduled to come every 8 to 10 minutes.
Monday–Friday 7 a.m.–6 p.m.

**Northwest Campus Shuttle**
The shuttle provides transportation across northern part of campus, with stops at Macgowan Hall, Kreiger Child Care Center, Southern Regional Library, and Hedrick Hall.
Monday–Friday 11:30 a.m.–2 p.m.

### Wilshire Center Shuttle

The shuttle makes a loop from Wilshire Center, with stops at Parking Structure 2, Gonda Research Facility, and 100 Medical Plaza.
Monday–Friday 7:30 a.m.–5:30 p.m.

## Public Transit

### Culver City Bus Lines

(310) 253-6500
www.culvercity.org/
Government/Transportation/
Bus.aspx
UCLA students can ride for half-price.

### Los Angeles Metropolitan Transit Authority

(800) COMMUTE
1 Gateway Plaza, Los Angeles
www.metro.net
UCLA students can get Go Metro, which allows half-price fare.

### Santa Monica Big Blue Bus

(310) 451-5444
www.bigbluebus.com/home/
index.asp
Students ride for a discounted rate with their BruinCard.

## Safety Escort Services

### Community Service Officer (CSO) Escorts

(310) 794-WALK
Daily 5 p.m.–1 a.m.

## Best Ways to Get to the Airport

A cab ride to the airport costs around $35.
During busy breaks, the UCLA Flyaway Service picks students up at 30-minute intervals during the day for $5. Shuttles drop students off at each LAX terminal.

## Nearest Airport

### Los Angeles International Airport

1 World Way, Los Angeles
(310) 646-5252
www.lawa.org/welcomeLAX.
aspx
The Los Angeles International Airport is 10 miles and approximately a 30-minute drive from UCLA.

## Nearest Passenger Bus

### Los Angeles Greyhound Station

1716 E. 7th St., Los Angeles
(213) 629-8401
www.greyhound.com
The station is approximately 16 miles from campus.

## Nearest Passenger Train

**Union Station**
800 N. Alameda St., Los Angeles
(800) 872-7245
*www.amtrak.com*
The station is approximately 17 miles from campus.

## Students Speak Out On...
# Transportation

### ℚ Transportation's Quick and Easy
UCLA provides a flyaway bus service to and from all the airports in the area for only $5. It comes at all times of the day and is so easy to use! There are also a variety of opportunities and programs available that make finding a ride home quick, affordable, and easy!

### ℚ Extremely Handy
Because UCLA is the biggest UC campus, there is actually a bus within the school that takes students from one side of campus to the other, and it's FREE! At the bus terminals, the buses wait patiently for some time so that students are able to board, and the fare is $1 compared to the usual $1.50. There are, of course, bus passes available for purchase for daily commuters.

### ℚ Transportation
The transportation within UCLA is good with its campus shuttle, as well as the outside buses. It is easy to get around if you know which bus to take.

### ℚ Big Blue Buses Are Great
A bike at UCLA is nice if you don't mind going up the hills. Everything is within walking distance, though. Buses take you anywhere from Westwood to Santa Monica for only a quarter if you show your BruinCard.

### ℚ No Car, Take the Bus
Public transportation is really good. There are buses that come often, and the cost is great for students who attend UCLA. We only have to pay a quarter when we show our student ID cards. For people who travel and come to

school late, we have a shuttle bus that picks students up where the bus leaves them. So it's really convenient for people to travel.

## Q Large Varieties of Transportation
There are many shuttles around the school that run between shopping centers, LAX airport, and school.

## Q Very Convenient Transportation
The bus schedules are pretty good. People mostly wait for only 15 minutes for each bus.

## Q Big Blue Bus
The Big Blue Bus system is great because there's a stop on campus, and it can take you almost anywhere around L.A. Fare is a quarter with your BruinCard.

# The College Prowler Take On...
## Transportation

With a swipe of the BruinCard, UCLA students can ride the bus for a quarter— enough said. The Big Blue Bus system whisks Bruins to venues from the beaches in Santa Monica to downtown shopping, and there is a stop nestled right at the edge of campus. Though the rides can be long and some schedules are unpredictable, the cost and range of the bus system look great when considering the alternative: LA traffic.

There is a reason why Los Angeles traffic is considered the worst in the nation. People refer to the freeways as "parking lots" during rush hour, and there is substantial traffic in the city practically every hour of the day. Because of these impediments, students are hesitant to use cars. Yet for hard-to-reach spots outside the bus system's bounds or daily jobs, driving is a necessity. And, most would agree that to experience LA in a non-touristy way, a car is a vital but hectic must-have.

**B**

The College Prowler® Grade on

Transportation: B

A high grade for Transportation indicates that campus buses, public buses, cabs, and rental cars are readily-available and affordable. Other determining factors include proximity to an airport and the necessity of transportation.

# Weather

### The Lowdown On...
## Weather

### Temperature Averages
Spring – High: 73 °F
Spring – Low: 55 °F
Summer – High: 83 °F
Summer – Low: 64 °F
Fall – High: 78 °F
Fall – Low: 59 °F
Winter – High: 69 °F
Winter – Low: 49 °F

### What to Pack
Comfy sandals for traversing
the huge campus
Sunglasses
Umbrella! Don't be fooled by
SoCal's reputation—it'll rain
when you least expect it.

### Precipitation Averages
Spring: 1.43 in.
Summer: 0.07 in.
Fall: 0.58 in.
Winter: 2.97 in.

### Students Speak Out On...
# Weather

### Q I Love LA
It is basically always sunny and 75 degrees climate-wise. It's the best place you can go to school.

### Q It's Usually Windy Weather.
The weather in LA is the best—it's almost always sunny, and when it's winter, it doesn't get too cold.

### Q Sunny and Clear
It's Los Angeles, enough said.

### Q Los Angeles Weather?
It's generally perfect: not too hot, not too cold. It's sunny Los Angeles, what can go wrong?

### Q What Weather?
It's SoCal . . . bad weather doesn't exist here.

### Q Motivating Sunshine!
It's sunny for the majority of the year, and that keeps me motivated and happy to go to class! At other schools, snow or cold might bog down my willpower to go to class or out to a party.

### Q Perfection
The weather is exactly what you'd expect from Southern California. It seems like it's 75 degrees almost every day. Even in the middle of winter, people are outside tanning and playing sports. Early fall and spring are the best because it's so nice outside all the time.

## ◯ It Doesn't Get Much Better

You can't complain with SoCal's sunshine. We get less than 20 days of rain per year, and you can wear shorts and flip-flops in the dead of winter.

The College Prowler Take On...
# Weather

UCLA students can peep outside their dorm window on any given day, and chances are it'll look like summertime. Welcome to the land of sun and sand, where locals shiver when the thermometer hits 65, and light rain is considered the ultimate disaster. The consistently warm weather makes some students nostalgic for the changing seasons back home, but most giddily embrace the thought of donning tank tops in January. A pleasant breeze is always drifting through the pines, and skies are rarely dotted with clouds. December through March can get chilly, but nothing more than a long-sleeved shirt or light sweater is required.

This never-ending perfection does have a drawback: distraction. For the first and last two months of the school year, the temptation to frolic by the rec center's pool can make getting to class a battle. And with Santa Monica's beaches a bus ride away, why would anyone show up for work? Yet, with a little planning and resolve, responsible Bruins find time to savor both the top-notch weather and educational opportunities at UCLA. They also bring rain boots—20 days of rain per year means 20 days of rain per year!

**A**

**The College Prowler® Grade on**

**Weather: A**

A high Weather grade designates that temperatures are mild and rarely reach extremes, that the campus tends to be sunny rather than rainy, and that weather is fairly consistent rather than unpredictable.

UCLA

# Report Card Summary

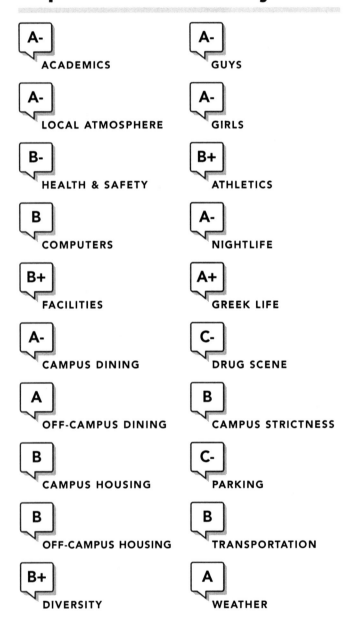

**A-** ACADEMICS

**A-** LOCAL ATMOSPHERE

**B-** HEALTH & SAFETY

**B** COMPUTERS

**B+** FACILITIES

**A-** CAMPUS DINING

**A** OFF-CAMPUS DINING

**B** CAMPUS HOUSING

**B** OFF-CAMPUS HOUSING

**B+** DIVERSITY

**A-** GUYS

**A-** GIRLS

**B+** ATHLETICS

**A-** NIGHTLIFE

**A+** GREEK LIFE

**C-** DRUG SCENE

**B** CAMPUS STRICTNESS

**C-** PARKING

**B** TRANSPORTATION

**A** WEATHER

# Overall Experience

**Students Speak Out On...**
## Overall Experience

### ♀ It's the Best

I can't imagine myself going anywhere other than UCLA. I am so proud to be a Bruin, and I love my school. Academically, it is a very challenging school, yet I've enjoyed every class I've taken, and studying doesn't feel like a chore but an interest. Socially, I love my fellow Bruins. There's always something to do and people to hang out with. I can't say I was ever bored. As far as opportunity, there are no limits to what a Bruin can do in life. To top it all off, our campus is absolutely gorgeous. I love UCLA!

## Q Awesomeness

UCLA is the best school ever. I love it here. There's a great balance of social and academic life. I'm so glad I chose to come here—it's made my college experience memorable.

## Q It's Been a Great Year of Life

I am learning so much that I am just in love with school. You can find everything you dream of.

## Q Best Choice I Ever Made

Going to UCLA was the best choice I ever made! It is a great party school, with outstanding academics. If you can juggle it all, then it's great!

## Q Amazing School

I absolutely love UCLA—it was by far the best choice for me and I'm so glad I made it. If you want to go out any given night of the week, you'll have no problem finding friends to go out with or places to go, but you also never have trouble finding people to stay in and study with. Everyone is fun and loves to party but has their acts together schoolwise (I mean come on, they did get in here).

## Q Best Decision I Ever Made!

UCLA is by far the best thing that has ever happened to me. The campus is beautiful, the teaching staff is world renowned, classes are hard but interesting and fulfilling, the student body is diverse, and there are more ways to get involved than you could even imagine! UCLA truly offers the quintessential college experience and I feel so blessed to be able to attend such a wonderful school!

## Q Students Make the UCLA Experience

People at UCLA make this experience as great as it is. Everyone is really diverse, balanced, and so nice. I love the people here.

# Q UCLA

It's a great school and a great campus. The people here are very diverse and easy to get along with. UCLA is only 30 minutes from the Santa Monica and Venice beaches (not including more). Plus, everything you possibly need is within a five-mile radius of the campus.

## The College Prowler Take On...
# Overall Experience

Smack dab in the middle of Los Angeles and on the list of America's top colleges, UCLA is a school for those who want to have a blast while focusing on schoolwork. Although course registration is a battle, classes are crowded, and the registrar is impersonal, students praise the wisdom of their professors and feel that a UCLA degree will open major doors in the job market. The quarter system moves fast and tests tend to sneak up stealthily, but this allows for more experimentation when choosing courses and far less boredom. With more than 100 majors to choose from, the campus is bustling with students of all ideologies, races, and academic interests, making rousing discussions an everyday experience.

One of the nation's few top-notch universities that isn't private, UCLA is a place for those who want to learn more than a textbook contains. There's pressure to shine socially and academically among the approximately 25,000 high-achieving Bruin undergrads, but there are plenty of campus organizations that give students a go-to friend group in the midst of the giant student body. However, it's up to the students to scout out and take advantage of all opportunities because nothing is handed to UCLA students—they must learn to navigate around red tape, persist through budget cuts, find parking and housing in Westwood's winding streets, and steer toward success. And how do they celebrate their successes? Parties! Whether through the semi-dominant Greek system or at a laid-back dorm gathering, UCLA students know how to put the books aside for a night. Overall, Bruins play nearly as hard as they work, making UCLA one of the most well-rounded schools imaginable.

# The Inside Scoop

### The Lowdown On...
## The Inside Scoop

### School Slang

**8 Clap**: The ultimate display of Bruin pride. The 8 Clap is performed simultaneously by thousands of students at sports events.

**Blackout**: The week before/during Greek rush periods, when the party scene is essentially dead

**BruCaf**: Bruin Café, the buzzing dorm eatery open until 2 a.m.

**Bruin Walk**: The central walkway that separates North Campus and South Campus

**Buck Fiddy's**: Student nickname for a food stand officially named Tommy Taco, which is a popular late-night nacho and fries hangout

**Cluster**: A group of classes that, when taken together, give credit for multiple general education classes in different subject areas (e.g. humanities, social sciences), and sometimes shave off extra classes students have to take

**The Dungeon**: Basement area of Powell Library (one of the quietest areas to study on campus)

**Midnight Yell**: Finals week tradition of screaming loudly one time at midnight to relieve stress

**North Campus Majors**: A nickname for social science and humanities majors, because most of these departments are located on the northern half of campus

**Rape Trail**: The (now) well-lit walkway between the dorms and the apartments

**South Campus Majors**: A nickname for life and physical science majors, because most of these departments are located on the southern half of campus

**Sunset**: All-encompassing term for the Sunset Canyon Recreation Center's field and two pools. Bikini-clad students swarm this area during spring quarter's warmer days.

**URSA**: The online enrollment system and infamous source of frustration over hard-to-find classes

**Wooden**: John Wooden Center, home of the ever-crowded gym

## Things I Wish I Knew Before Coming To School

• Even the people who appear to party 24/7 study, so you should too.

• Get the 14 Premier Meal Plan. It has the perfect amount of meals and extras.

• Get your own bed linens (twin extra-long for dorm beds).

• Go to the frats during Orientation Week.

• If you're going to drink illegally, don't be loud about it.

• Some of the teachers are more interesting than the subjects they teach.

• Someone in the dorms will have a microwave (and it's best if it's not you).

• Visit the Career Center often to avoid being unemployed directly out of college.

• Weekends should be used for getting away to local wilderness areas.

• Your grades will plummet if you party more than you study.

## Tips to Succeed
- Actually go to class.
- Always dispute bad grades.
- Appear interested (even if you're not).
- Ask the TAs tons of questions.
- Buy your books online to avoid paying zillions at the campus bookstore.
- Check your e-mail frequently.
- Don't ever fall behind—the quarter system moves fast.
- Drink lots of coffee!
- Go to office hours.
- Pick classes you actually like.
- Research your professors before choosing your classes.
- Study with other people in the class.

## Traditions
**Basketball Campout**: Tents are pitched and pizza is ordered outside Pauley Pavilion on nights before big basketball games as students stake out for the best seats.

**Book Reading Marathon**: This little jewel is an English-lover's delight, as the Undergraduate English Association sponsors a reading of a book in 15-minute increments. Many times, actors will come out to read the first hour of the book and support the English department.

**Dance Marathon**: Each winter, hundreds of Bruins subject themselves to 26 hours of constant dancing in Ackerman Grand Ballroom to raise funds for pediatric AIDS. Celebrity appearances and killer food sponsors are highlights.

**Inverted Fountain**: All UCLA students are only supposed to touch the fountain twice in their entire UCLA career: during orientation and on graduation day (assuming you remember). The fountain ushers all students into the University and bids them adieu, as well. It is a time-honored tradition that links all UCLA alumni.

**Undie Run**: On the final night of each quarter, students strip to their knickers for a speedy jaunt around Westwood and through campus. Though cops have been cracking down on the event lately, a hundred or so brave souls have kept it rolling.

## Urban Legends

• Some say the Inverted Fountain, which was designed by a USC grad, was made to look like a toilet when viewing the fountain with Franz Hall in the background.

## Students Speak Out On...
# The Inside Scoop

### ℚ UCLA Has So Many Programs

There are so many programs for anything you want to do at UCLA, and it's in LA, so you have access to urban neighborhoods if you want to do urban planning. There's Hollywood if you want to do movies, there are museums if you want to do art, and our medical center is ranked third in the nation. There are so many opportunities to do anything.

### ℚ Great Location

Being in the middle of Los Angeles allows for so many incredible off-campus activities. The public transportation system is great if you don't have a car, and you can get pretty much anywhere for almost nothing.

### ℚ The Bruin Spirit

Everyone here is so happy to be! We have our own legends, traditions, and superstitions. No matter what your interests are, whether you are "North" (humanities) or "South" (sciences) Campus major, you will find your niche among the various activities and services offered to you here at UCLA.

### ℚ GE Clusters

These are open to college freshmen, and they last a year. It is a class that you take, and at the end of the year, instead of only receiving three GE credits, you get four, plus a writing requirement. They are really good to knock out classes in subject areas that are less interesting to you.

## Q Helping Out is Popular

There's so much volunteerism on campus. From going abroad to Africa to tutoring at inner-city schools, everyone wants to get involved and does.

## Q We're Famous!

A lot of movies and commercials are filmed here, so it's fun to see your school on TV! That also means we have really cool architecture. And unlike real movie stars, everyone here is pretty friendly. I didn't expect that.

## Q Clubs

There are clubs for everyone, and they actually make a difference. If you like to read, there is a club for you. There are other clubs for community service, technology, MAC users, or environmental concerns. Anything and everything is available to you.

## Q Diversity

My school is one of the most diverse schools in the nation, with people from all sorts of demographics of the United States and from all over the world.

# Jobs &
# Internships

**The Lowdown On...**
## Jobs & Internships

### Career Center
**501 Westwood Plaza**
(310) 206-1915
*career.ucla.edu*

### Employment Services?
Yes

### Placement Services?
Yes

### Other Career Services
BruinView, online job and
internship database
Career counseling
Career fairs
Career lab with a library of
resources
Employer information
sessions
Internship & International
Opportunities (program to
help students find openings)
Letter of reference services
Networking opportunities
On-campus job interviews

Résumé critique
Salary comparison
Workshops

## Advice

Finding on-campus work is simple—popular jobs include coffee houses, the rec center's outdoor pool, and campus tours. The pay isn't fabulous, but some students work as part of their financial aid package and certainly reap the reward. Off-campus employment is a little trickier to secure, but one of Los Angeles' glittering promises is its internship and job spectrum. Savvy applicants can find spots in the city's bustling entertainment industry and UCLA's top-notch medical facilities. BruinView is an online portal that allows students to upload their résumé, which is circulated to companies specifically seeking Bruin interns. The Career Center is also a handy resource with its résumé workshops, mock interviews, and friendly counselors.

## Firms That Most Frequently Hire Grads

Amgen
Blizzard Entertainment
Broadcom
Cisco Systems
Deloitte Touche
Eli Lilly
Enterprise Rent-A-Car
FTI Consulting
General Motors
Goldman Sachs
Kaplan
KPMG
Lockheed Martin
Macy's
Neiman Marcus
Northrop Grumman
PricewaterhouseCoopers
The Princeton Review
Raytheon
Shimmick Construction
Southwestern Company
Target Corporation
Teledyne Scientific & Imaging
Towers Watson

Vector Marketing
ViaSat
Wal-Mart

## Did You Know?

Best On-Campus Jobs:

- One of campus's three coffeehouses
- Lifeguarding at Sunset Recreation Center
- The Wooden Center (gym) desk
- Campus tour guide

Worst On-Campus Jobs:

- The bookstore
- Dining Services
- The library

Best Off-Campus Jobs (In Westwood):

- Coffeehouses like Starbucks or Peet's Coffee
- Movie theaters (you might catch a premiere!)
- Boutiques
- UCLA Medical Center (if you're an ambitious pre-med student)

# Alumni & Post-Grads

### The Lowdown On...
## Alumni & Post-Grads

### Alumni Office
**UCLA Alumni Association**
James West Alumni Center,
325 Westwood Plaza
Phone: (800) 825-2586
Fax: (310) 825-8678
*alumni@UCLAlumni.net*
*www.UCLAlumni.net*

### Major Alumni Events
Beat 'SC – The night before
the anticipated USC football
matchup, students and
alumni crowd the intramural
field for a humongous bonfire
and a pep talk by the coach.
Blue and Gold Week – The
Student Alumni Association
pumps up the Bruin
student body with events,
performances, and flat-out
spirit to gear up for the big
football game against USC
during this week of wildness.
Dinners for 12 Strangers
– With the goal of new
friendships and networking,
a blend of alums and current
students gather at these
dinners held at the homes of

alumni.

Spring Sing – Students, alumni, and faculty all come to watch this annual singing showdown. Some past performers have become national recording artists, including Sara Bareilles and Maroon 5.

## Services Available

Alumni career network
Alumni dinner parties
Alumni travel program
Career counseling and workshops
Discount on medical procedures like Lasik surgery, plastic surgery, and hair restoration
Discount rate at various Starwood and Club Quarters hotels
Discounts at Beverly Hilton
Discounts on auto, home, renter's, and health insurance
Library and online library privileges
Online directory
Permanent e-mail forwarding
Recreational facilities privileges
Two-for-one season football tickets
UCLA credit and debit cards (through Bank of America)

## Alumni Publications

UCLA Magazine

## Did You Know?

Famous UCLA Alumni:

• Kareem Abdul-Jabbar – Legendary basketball player
  • Troy Aikman – Star NFL quarterback
  • Nancy Cartwright – Voice of Bart Simpson on "The Simpsons"
• Jimmy Connors – World tennis champion
• Francis Ford Coppola – Filmmaker; director of the "Godfather" trilogy
• James Dean – '50s actor and star of "Rebel Without a Cause"
• James Franco – Star of the "Spiderman" trilogy
• Andrew Goldberg – Contributing writer for the TV show "Family Guy"
• Karch Kiraly – Professional volleyball player; three-time Olympic gold medalist
• Jim Morrison – Rock idol and frontman for The Doors
• John Soloman – Writer for "Saturday Night Live"
• Darren Star – Creator of "Sex and the City," "Melrose Place," and "Beverly Hills, 90210"

# Student Organizations

**The Lowdown On...**

## Clubs and Organizations on Campus

On a campus as large as UCLA's, you will encounter hundreds of student groups trying to make their mark. Most students join a club or organization of some sort in search of a niche among UCLA's 25,000 undergrads, and community service organizations are popular. The Student Alumni Association, composed of fun-loving Bruins, is very active and plans well-respected events like Spring Sing and Homecoming that attract current students and alumni. The Dance Marathon committee is also a somewhat "trendy" service group to join.

## Student Organizations Web Site

*www.studentgroups.ucla.edu*

## ROTC

Air Force ROTC: Yes
Navy ROTC: Yes
Army ROTC: Yes

## Student Newspaper

The Daily Bruin: *www. dailybruin.com*

## Student Activities Offered

Campus ministries
Choral groups
Concert band
Dance
Drama/theater
International student organization
Jazz band
Literary magazine
Marching band
Model UN
Music ensembles
Musical theater
Opera
Pep band
Radio station
Student government
Student newspaper
Student-run film society
Symphony orchestra
Television station
Yearbook

# The Best

## The BEST Things

1. Awesome food in dining halls and off campus

2. Location in LA and its close proximity to beaches

3. 60-degree winters

4. Movie premieres in Westwood and seeing actors on campus

5. Making friends from diverse backgrounds

6. Quarter system

7. Midnight food runs at the dorms

8. Architecture on campus

9. Great basketball team

10. UCLA's prestige

# The Worst

## The **WORST** Things

**1.** No parking!

**2.** Traffic

**3.** Smog

**4.** Stupid school politics

**5.** Student body size

**6.** High-priced Westwood apartments

**7.** Need a car to go out at night

**8.** High curves from smart people

**9.** Rundown dorms

**10.** Classes fill up so fast

# Visiting

### The Lowdown On...
## Visiting

### Campus Tours

General campus tours led by students are available between one and three times daily, depending on the season, and last about two hours. Reservations are required at least three to four weeks ahead of time. Reservations can be made at www.admissions.ucla.edu/Prospect/tours.htm. The Housing Office also offers tours of the on-campus housing facilities Monday through Friday at 12:30 p.m. Reservations are required and can be made by e-mailing hao@ha.ucla.edu or calling (310) 825-4271.

### Campus Map

*maps.ucla.edu/campus*

## Virtual Tour of Campus

*www.admissions.ucla.edu/selfguidedtour/default.htm*

## Interviews & Information Sessions

Interviews are not used for admission into UCLA. For information on admissions or other aspects of the University, you can sign up for a Recruitment Information Session. Call the UCLA Undergraduate Admissions Office at during business hours Monday through Friday for more information.

## Overnight Visits

The Regents Scholar Society offers an overnight stay program for potential Bruins to tour campus and live like a student for a night. The program is offered on four weekends in April. Visit www.rssla.org/outreach/osp for details.

# Words to Know

**Academic Probation** – A suspension imposed on a student if he or she fails to keep up with the school's minimum academic requirements. Those unable to improve their grades after receiving this warning can face dismissal.

**Beer Pong/Beirut** – A drinking game involving cups of beer arranged in a pyramid shape on each side of a table. The goal is to get a ping pong ball into one of the opponent's cups by throwing the ball or hitting it with a paddle. If the ball lands in a cup, the opponent is required to drink the beer.

**Bid** – An invitation from a fraternity or sorority to 'pledge' (join) that specific house.

**Blue-Light Phone** – Brightly-colored phone posts with a blue light bulb on top. These phones exist for security purposes and are located at various outside locations around most campuses. In an emergency, a student can pick up one of these phones (free of charge) to connect with campus police or a security escort.

**Campus Police** – Police who are specifically assigned to a given institution. Campus police are typically not regular city officers; they are employed by the university in a full-time capacity.

**Club Sports** – A level of sports that falls somewhere between varsity and intramural. If a student is unable to commit to a varsity team but has a lot of passion for athletics, a club sport could be a better, less intense option. Even less demanding, intramural (IM) sports often involve no traveling and considerably less time.

**Cocaine** – An illegal drug. Also known as "coke" or "blow," cocaine often resembles a white crystalline or powdery substance. It is highly addictive and dangerous.

**Common Application** – An application with which students can apply to multiple schools.

**Course Registration** – The period of official class selection for the upcoming quarter or semester. Prior to registration, it is best to prepare several back-up courses in case a particular class becomes full. If a course is full, students can place themselves on the waitlist, although this still does not guarantee entry.

**Division Athletics** – Athletic classifications range from Division I to Division III. Division IA is the most competitive, while Division III is considered to be the least competitive.

**Dorm** – A dorm (or dormitory) is an on-campus housing facility. Dorms can provide a range of options from suite-style rooms to more communal options that include shared bathrooms. Most first-year students live in dorms. Some upperclassmen who wish to stay on campus also choose this option.

**Early Action** – An application option with which a student can apply to a school and receive an early acceptance response without a binding commitment. This system is becoming less and less available.

**Early Decision** – An application option that students should use only if they are certain they plan to attend the school in question. If a student applies using the early decision option and is admitted, he or she is required and bound to attend that university. Admission rates are usually higher among students who apply through early decision, as the student is clearly indicating that the school is his or her first choice.

**Ecstasy** – An illegal drug. Also known as "E" or "X," ecstasy looks like a pill and most resembles an aspirin. Considered a party drug, ecstasy is very dangerous and can be deadly.

**Ethernet** – An extremely fast Internet connection available in most university-owned residence halls. To use an Ethernet connection properly, a student will need a network card and cable for his or her computer.

**Fake ID** – A counterfeit identification card that contains false information. Most commonly, students get fake IDs with altered birthdates so that they appear to be older than 21 (and therefore of legal drinking age). Even though it is illegal, many college students have fake IDs in hopes of purchasing alcohol or getting into bars.

**Frosh** – Slang for "freshman" or "freshmen."

**Hazing** – Initiation rituals administered by some fraternities or sororities as part of the pledging process. Many universities have outlawed hazing due to its degrading, and sometimes dangerous, nature.

**Intramurals (IMs)** – A popular, and usually free, sport league in which students create teams and compete against one another. These sports vary in competitiveness and can include a range of activities—everything from billiards to water polo. IM sports are a great way to meet people with similar interests.

**Keg** – Officially called a half-barrel, a keg contains roughly 200 12-ounce servings of beer.

**LSD** – An illegal drug, also known as acid, this hallucinogenic drug most commonly resembles a tab of paper.

**Marijuana** – An illegal drug, also known as weed or pot; along with alcohol, marijuana is one of the most commonly found drugs on campuses across the country.

**Major** –The focal point of a student's college studies; a specific topic that is studied for a degree. Examples of majors include physics, English, history, computer science, economics, business, and music. Many students decide on a specific major before arriving on campus, while others are simply "undecided" until declaring a major. Those who are extremely interested in two areas can also choose to double major.

**Meal Block** – The equivalent of one meal. Students on a meal plan usually receive a fixed number of meals per week. Each meal, or "block," can be redeemed at the school's dining facilities in place of cash. Often, a student's weekly allotment of meal blocks will be forfeited if not used.

**Minor** – An additional focal point in a student's education. Often serving as a complement or addition to a student's main area of focus, a minor has fewer requirements and prerequisites to fulfill than a major. Minors are not required for graduation from most schools; however some students who want to explore many different interests choose to pursue both a major and a minor.

**Mushrooms** – An illegal drug. Also known as "'shrooms," this drug resembles regular mushrooms but is extremely hallucinogenic.

**Off-Campus Housing** – Housing from a particular landlord or rental group that is not affiliated with the university. Depending on the college, off-campus housing can range from extremely popular to non-existent. Students who choose to live off campus are typically given more freedom, but they also have to deal with possible subletting scenarios, furniture, bills, and other issues. In addition to these factors, rental prices and distance often affect a student's decision to move off campus.

**Office Hours** – Time that teachers set aside for students who have questions about coursework. Office hours are a good forum for students to go over any problems and to show interest in the subject material.

**Pledging** – The early phase of joining a fraternity or sorority, pledging takes place after a student has gone through rush and received a bid. Pledging usually lasts between one and two semesters. Once the pledging period is complete and a particular student has done everything that is required to become a member, that student is considered a brother or sister. If a fraternity or a sorority would decide to "haze" a group of students, this initiation would take place during the pledging period.

**Private Institution** – A school that does not use tax revenue to subsidize education costs. Private schools typically cost more than public schools and are usually smaller.

**Prof** – Slang for "professor."

**Public Institution** – A school that uses tax revenue to subsidize education costs. Public schools are often a good value for in-state residents and tend to be larger than most private colleges.

**Quarter System** (or Trimester System) – A type of academic calendar system. In this setup, students take classes for three academic periods. The first quarter usually starts in late September or early October and concludes right before Christmas. The second quarter usually starts around early to mid–January and finishes up around March or April. The last academic quarter, or "third quarter," usually starts in late March or early April and finishes up in late May or Mid-June. The fourth quarter is summer. The major difference between the quarter system and semester system is that students take more, less comprehensive courses under the quarter calendar.

**RA** (Resident Assistant) – A student leader who is assigned to a particular floor in a dormitory in order to help to the other students who live there. An RA's duties include ensuring student safety and providing assistance wherever possible.

**Recitation** – An extension of a specific course; a review session. Some classes, particularly large lectures, are supplemented with mandatory recitation sessions that provide a relatively personal class setting.

**Rolling Admissions** – A form of admissions. Most commonly found at public institutions, schools with this type of policy continue to accept students throughout the year until their class sizes are met. For example, some schools begin accepting students as early as December and will continue to do so until April or May.

**Room and Board** – This figure is typically the combined cost of a university-owned room and a meal plan.

**Room Draw/Housing Lottery** – A common way to pick on-campus room assignments for the following year. If a student decides to remain in university-owned housing, he or she is assigned a unique number that, along with seniority, is used to determine his or her housing for the next year.

**Rush** – The period in which students can meet the brothers and sisters of a particular chapter and find out if a given fraternity or sorority is right for them. Rushing a fraternity or a sorority is not a requirement at any school. The goal of rush is to give students who are serious about pledging a feel for what to expect.

**Semester System** – The most common type of academic calendar system at college campuses. This setup typically includes two semesters in a given school year. The fall semester starts around the end of August or early September and concludes before winter vacation. The spring semester usually starts in mid-January and ends in late April or May.

**Student Center/Rec Center/Student Union** – A common area on campus that often contains study areas, recreation facilities, and eateries. This building is often a good place to meet up with fellow students; depending on the school, the student center can have a huge role or a non-existent role in campus life.

**Student ID** – A university-issued photo ID that serves as a student's key to school-related functions. Some schools require students to show these cards in order to get into dorms, libraries, cafeterias, and other facilities. In addition to storing meal plan information, in some cases, a student ID can actually work as a debit card and allow students to purchase things from bookstores or local shops.

**Suite** – A type of dorm room. Unlike dorms that feature communal bathrooms shared by the entire floor, suites offer bathrooms shared only among the suite. Suite-style dorm rooms can house anywhere from two to ten students.

**TA** (Teacher's Assistant) – An undergraduate or grad student who helps in some manner with a specific course. In some cases, a TA will teach a class, assist a professor, grade assignments, or conduct office hours.

**Undergraduate** – A student in the process of studying for his or her bachelor's degree.

## About the Author

**Name:** Suzy Strutner

**Hometown:** Newport Beach, Calif.

**Major:** Communication Studies

**Fun Fact:** During finals week, Suzy once consumed 12 muffins from Bruin Café.

**Previous Contributors:** Erik Robert Flegal

# Pros and Cons

Still can't figure out if this is the right school for you?
You've already read through this in-depth guide;
why not list the pros and cons? It will really help
with narrowing down your decision and determining
whether or not this school is right for you.

| Pros | Cons |
| --- | --- |
| ..................................... | ..................................... |
| ..................................... | ..................................... |
| ..................................... | ..................................... |
| ..................................... | ..................................... |
| ..................................... | ..................................... |
| ..................................... | ..................................... |
| ..................................... | ..................................... |
| ..................................... | ..................................... |
| ..................................... | ..................................... |
| ..................................... | ..................................... |
| ..................................... | ..................................... |
| ..................................... | ..................................... |

# Pros and Cons

Still can't figure out if this is the right school for you?
You've already read through this in-depth guide;
why not list the pros and cons? It will really help
with narrowing down your decision and determining
whether or not this school is right for you.

| Pros | Cons |
|------|------|
| ..................................... | ..................................... |
| ..................................... | ..................................... |
| ..................................... | ..................................... |
| ..................................... | ..................................... |
| ..................................... | ..................................... |
| ..................................... | ..................................... |
| ..................................... | ..................................... |
| ..................................... | ..................................... |
| ..................................... | ..................................... |
| ..................................... | ..................................... |
| ..................................... | ..................................... |
| ..................................... | ..................................... |

# Notes

....................................................................
....................................................................
....................................................................
....................................................................
....................................................................
....................................................................
....................................................................
....................................................................
....................................................................
....................................................................
....................................................................
....................................................................
....................................................................
....................................................................
....................................................................

# Notes

......................................................................
......................................................................
......................................................................
......................................................................
......................................................................
......................................................................
......................................................................
......................................................................
......................................................................
......................................................................
......................................................................
......................................................................
......................................................................
......................................................................
......................................................................

# Notes

......................................................................
......................................................................
......................................................................
......................................................................
......................................................................
......................................................................
......................................................................
......................................................................
......................................................................
......................................................................
......................................................................
......................................................................
......................................................................
......................................................................
......................................................................

# Notes

........................................................

........................................................

........................................................

........................................................

........................................................

........................................................

........................................................

........................................................

........................................................

........................................................

........................................................

........................................................

........................................................

........................................................

........................................................

# College Scholarships

## *Search. Apply. Win!*

College Prowler gives away thousands of dollars each month through our popular monthly scholarships, including our $2,000 "No Essay" scholarship.

Plus, we'll connect you with hundreds of other scholarships based on your unique information and qualifications!

Create a College Prowler account today to get matched with millions of dollars in relevant scholarships!

**Sign up and apply now at**
**_www.collegeprowler.com/register_**

WWW.COLLEGEPROWLER.COM

# Review Your School!

## *Let your voice be heard.*

Every year, thousands of students take our online survey to share their opinions about campus life.

Now's your chance to help millions of high school students choose the right college for them.

Tell us what life is really like at your school by taking our online survey or even uploading your own photos and videos!

And as our thanks to you for participating in our survey, we'll enter you into a random drawing for our $1,000 Monthly Survey Scholarship!

**For more information, check out**
**_www.collegeprowler.com/survey_**

WWW.COLLEGEPROWLER.COM

# Write For Us!

## *Express your opinion. Get published!*

Interested in being a published author? College Prowler is always on the lookout for current college students across the country to write the guides for their schools.

The contributing author position is a unique opportunity for eager college students to bolster their résumés and portfolios, become published authors both online and in print, and gain tremendous exposure to millions of high school students nationwide.

**For more details, visit**
***www.collegeprowler.com/careers***

Albion College
Alfred University
Allegheny College
Alverno College
American Intercontinental
University Online
American University
Amherst College
Arizona State University
Ashford University
The Art Institute of
California – Orange
County
Auburn University
Austin College
Babson College
Ball State University
Bard College
Barnard College
Barry University
Baruch College
Bates College
Bay Path College
Baylor University
Beloit College
Bentley University
Berea College
Binghamton University
Birmingham Southern
College
Bob Jones University
Boston College
Boston University
Bowdoin College
Bradley University
Brandeis University
Brigham Young University
Brigham Young
University – Idaho
Brown University
Bryant University
Bryn Mawr College
Bucknell University
Cal Poly Pomona
California College
of the Arts
California Institute
of Technology
California Polytechnic
State University
California State University
– Monterey Bay
California State University
– Northridge
California State University
– San Marcos
Carleton College
Carnegie Mellon University
Case Western Reserve
University
Catawba College
Catholic University
of America

Centenary College
of Louisiana
Centre College
Chapman University
Chatham University
City College of New York
City College of
San Francisco
Claflin University
Claremont McKenna
College
Clark Atlanta University
Clark University
Clemson University
Cleveland State University
Colby College
Colgate University
College of Charleston
College of Mount
Saint Vincent
College of Notre
Dame of Maryland
College of the Holy Cross
College of William & Mary
College of Wooster
Colorado College
Columbia College Chicago
Columbia University
Concordia University
– Wisconsin
Connecticut College
Contra Costa College
Cornell College
Cornell University
Creighton University
CUNY Lehman College
CUNY Queens College
CUNY Queensborough
Community College
Dalton State College
Dartmouth College
Davidson College
De Anza College
Del Mar College
Denison University
DePaul University
DePauw University
Diablo Valley College
Dickinson College
Dordt College
Drexel University
Duke University
Duquesne University
Earlham College
East Carolina University
Eckerd College
El Paso Community
College
Elon University
Emerson College
Emory University
Fashion Institute of Design
& Merchandising

Fashion Institute of
Technology
Ferris State University
Florida Atlantic University
Florida Southern College
Florida State University
Fordham University
Franklin & Marshall
College
Franklin Pierce University
Frederick Community
College
Freed-Hardeman
University
Furman University
Gannon University
Geneva College
George Mason University
George Washington
University
Georgetown University
Georgia Institute of
Technology
Georgia Perimeter College
Georgia State University
Germanna Community
College
Gettysburg College
Gonzaga University
Goucher College
Grinnell College
Grove City College
Guilford College
Gustavus Adolphus
College
Hamilton College
Hampshire College
Hampton University
Hanover College
Harvard University
Harvey Mudd College
Hastings College
Haverford College
Hillsborough Community
College
Hofstra University
Hollins University
Howard University
Hunter College (CUNY)
Idaho State University
Illinois State University
Illinois Wesleyan University
Indiana Univ.–Purdue Univ.
Indianapolis (IUPUI)
Indiana University
Iowa State University
Ithaca College
Jackson State University
James Madison University
Johns Hopkins University
Juniata College
Kansas State University
Kaplan University

Kent State University
Kenyon College
La Roche College
Lafayette College
Lawrence University
Lehigh University
Lewis & Clark College
Linfield College
Los Angeles City College
Los Angeles Valley College
Louisiana College
Louisiana State University
Loyola College in
Maryland
Loyola Marymount
University
Loyola University Chicago
Luther College
Macalester College
Macomb Community
College
Manhattan College
Manhattanville College
Marlboro College
Marquette University
Maryville University
Massachusetts College
of Art & Design
Massachusetts Institute
of Technology
McGill University
Merced College
Mercyhurst College
Messiah College
Miami University
Michigan State University
Middle Tennessee
State University
Middlebury College
Millsaps College
Minnesota State
University – Moorhead
Missouri State University
Montana State University
Montclair State University
Moorpark College
Mount Holyoke College
Muhlenberg College
New College of Florida
New York University
North Carolina A&T
State University
North Carolina State
University
Northeastern University
Northern Arizona
University
Northern Illinois University
Northwest Florida
State College
Northwestern College
– Saint Paul
Northwestern University

Oakwood University
Oberlin College
Occidental College
Oglethorpe University
Ohio State University
Ohio University
Ohio Wesleyan University
Old Dominion University
Onondaga Community College
Oral Roberts University
Pace University
Palm Beach State College
Penn State Altoona
Penn State Brandywine
Penn State University
Pepperdine University
Pitzer College
Pomona College
Princeton University
Providence College
Purdue University
Radford University
Ramapo College of New Jersey
Reed College
Rensselaer Polytechnic Institute
Rhode Island School of Design
Rhodes College
Rice University
Rider University
Robert Morris University
Rochester Institute of Technology
Rocky Mountain College of Art & Design
Rollins College
Rowan University
Rutgers University
Sacramento State
Saint Francis University
Saint Joseph's University
Saint Leo University
Salem College
Salisbury University
Sam Houston State University
Samford University
San Diego State University
San Francisco State University
Santa Clara University
Santa Fe College
Sarah Lawrence College
Scripps College
Seattle University
Seton Hall University
Simmons College
Skidmore College
Slippery Rock University
Smith College

South Texas College
Southern Methodist University
Southwestern University
Spelman College
St. John's College – Annapolis
St. John's University
St. Louis University
St. Mary's University
St. Olaf College
Stanford University
State University of New York – Purchase College
State University of New York at Fredonia
State University of New York at Oswego
Stetson University
Stevens-Henager College
Stony Brook University (SUNY)
Susquehanna University
Swarthmore College
Syracuse University
Taylor University
Temple University
Tennessee State University
Texas A&M University
Texas Christian University
Texas Tech
The Community College of Baltimore County
Towson University
Trinity College (Conn.)
Trinity University (Texas)
Troy University
Truman State University
Tufts University
Tulane University
Union College
University at Albany (SUNY)
University at Buffalo (SUNY)
University of Alabama
University of Arizona
University of Arkansas
University of Arkansas at Little Rock
University of California – Berkeley
University of California – Davis
University of California – Irvine
University of California – Los Angeles
University of California – Merced
University of California – Riverside
University of California – San Diego

University of California – Santa Barbara
University of California – Santa Cruz
University of Central Florida
University of Chicago
University of Cincinnati
University of Colorado
University of Connecticut
University of Delaware
University of Denver
University of Florida
University of Georgia
University of Hartford
University of Illinois
University of Illinois at Chicago
University of Iowa
University of Kansas
University of Kentucky
University of Louisville
University of Maine
University of Maryland
University of Maryland – Baltimore County
University of Massachusetts
University of Miami
University of Michigan
University of Minnesota
University of Mississippi
University of Missouri
University of Montana
University of Mount Union
University of Nebraska
University of Nevada – Las Vegas
University of New Hampshire
University of North Carolina
University of North Carolina – Greensboro
University of Notre Dame
University of Oklahoma
University of Oregon
University of Pennsylvania
University of Phoenix
University of Pittsburgh
University of Puget Sound
University of Rhode Island
University of Richmond
University of Rochester
University of San Diego
University of San Francisco
University of South Carolina
University of South Dakota
University of South Florida
University of Southern California
University of St Thomas – Texas

University of Tampa
University of Tennessee
University of Tennessee at Chattanooga
University of Texas
University of Utah
University of Vermont
University of Virginia
University of Washington
University of Western Ontario
University of Wisconsin
University of Wisconsin – Stout
Urbana University
Ursinus College
Valencia Community College
Valparaiso University
Vanderbilt University
Vassar College
Villanova University
Virginia Commonwealth University
Virginia Tech
Virginia Union University
Wagner College
Wake Forest University
Warren Wilson College
Washington & Jefferson College
Washington & Lee University
Washington University in St. Louis
Wellesley College
Wesleyan University
West Los Angeles College
West Point Military Academy
West Virginia University
Western Illinois University
Western Kentucky University
Wheaton College (Ill.)
Wheaton College (Mass.)
Whitman College
Whitworth University
Wilkes University
Willamette University
Williams College
Xavier University
Yale University
Youngstown State University